Under Fate's Wing

Under Fate's Wing

A Refugee Girl's Flight to Freedom in the Shadows of World War II

Hillevi Ruumet

Syncronea Publications
Ashland, Oregon

Book design by Ray Rhamey

Cover by Berkeley Fuller-Lewis
Cover image adapted from Will Milne via https//stocksnap.io

ISBN 978-0-9966987-0-2

Library of Congress Control Number 2015915198

creative non-fiction, memoir, women and children in World War II

DEDICATION

IN MEMORY OF
MY EXTRAORDINARY PARENTS

LEO AND HERTA RUUMET

Contents

PREFACE

Under Fate's Wing was originally intended for the next generations of my family, so that the heroism and humanity of my parents, and others of their generation, would serve as a legacy for their future.

Then I began to read more about refugees displaced by World War II and discovered that when the war ended there were 1.8 million others like us from the Eastern European countries who could not go back home. As "collateral damage" of a conflict they had no part in, they had lost their homelands to the Soviet Union and faced execution or slow death in Stalin's Gulag if they returned. The numbers shocked me. I had assumed thousands, but not millions.

In my search for deeper understanding, I found very little written that would have given the reader a live sense of such an experience. No wonder most people today are not even aware we existed.

If they are, they have no way of identifying with the full reality of the emotional devastation in post-war Europe, especially of ordinary people who had lost absolutely everything that had been their life and now faced an unknown future as unwelcome, stateless refugees adrift in a foreign land.

This made me realize that my story is a window into a fading past that warrants a place in written history, especially in view of the unspeakable violence that is escalating once more, with millions dead or displaced in a world that seems addicted to warfare.

So many of them are children like I was, and the media, today as they did then, tend to focus on military exploits and horror stories but neglect the mass destruction of real lives, of people who never rise to public visibility except as part of an abstract statistic.

The intent of this memoir is to shine a retrospective light on one such family's wartime and postwar experiences of tragedy and triumph, through the young eyes of the girl who lived it.

Ashland, Oregon
July 21, 2015

PART I
EXILE

Chapter 1

UPROOTED

September 21, 1944 was an ordinary autumn day in Tallinn, Estonia—and the end of my world.

We had spent much of the night huddling in the cellar while Russian warplanes blanket-bombed the city. When we emerged into the eerie morning stillness, a decision had been made that terrified me even more than the bombs.

That afternoon, while my parents were too busy to notice, I slipped away to my secret refuge in their bedroom, behind Mother's mahogany dressing table with its smooth, shiny surface that I loved to touch. I loved to watch her as she sat on the brocade-covered stool to put on makeup and comb her hair, loved to secretly sniff her perfume bottles, almost empty now. I adored Mother and wanted to grow up to be just like her.

Set diagonally across the far corner of the room, its high full-width mirror left barely enough room on one side for me to squeeze in behind. Shivering, I curled my six-year-old body into a ball in the corner.

They would never find me here, I thought, and they wouldn't leave without me. If I could only stay hidden long enough, we wouldn't have to go.

I was determined to grow up in the only home I knew, but something really bad called war had turned our lives upside down. Rushing down into the cellar to hide from falling bombs had become a regular event. German soldiers were everywhere.

Two had seized our German shepherd Toby, who patiently pulled my sled around the garden every winter. He would be a good soldier, they said, and took him away. Our small black-and-white dog had already disappeared, and I was sure something bad had happened to him. Trying to imagine a good life for him somewhere else didn't work.

My only other playmate was "Ome"—the Other Me behind the mirror. I didn't want to leave her either. I was an only child. Who else would be there for me when I needed a friend? Everything I loved was slipping away. I wanted my life before the war back, but my parents said the Russian army was approaching Tallinn. If we stayed we'd be sent to a terrible place called Siberia, where lots of people died. We had to leave and go to Sweden where we'd be safe.

When the Russians had occupied us before, they took Aunt Ida with her husband and three sons away to Siberia, and that would happen to us if we stayed. Their two daughters were lucky not to be home when the soldiers came, and escaped to Stockholm after the rest of the family was taken.

We would be living near them when we got there, Mother said, but that was no comfort.

I heard Father come into the bedroom calling my name. I held my breath. Then I heard him leave and relaxed in relief—but almost immediately, his voice came again, close to my ear through the opening I thought was my secret:

"There you are! What on earth are you doing? We have to leave right now." He looked more sad than angry.

"Go find your doll if you want to take her with you," he added softly.

"We'll come back soon, won't we?"

I was desperate. There was no way out now.

"I hope so, dear child. I hope so."

His tone and sad eyes said he didn't really believe it. Too devastated even to cry, I whispered goodbye to Ome in the mirror and promised I'd come back soon. I *would*.

Father's voice was gentle as he touched my shoulder.

"You have to be brave. You're such a smart girl. This is the only way we can all be safe."

With shaky legs, I got my favorite doll and followed him to the foyer where Mother and my grandmother waited with our suitcases. "Mamma" had lived with us since I was born, and she was coming with us. It was because of her that we could go to Sweden. Her father was Swedish, so she had managed to get entry documents for all of us.

Only one suitcase per person was allowed on the ship, so we could only take basic necessities and a few treasured mementoes. Mother, with her nine-month pregnant belly and limited ability to carry bags, held my hand tightly as we piled into a waiting taxi and sped to Tallinn Harbor.

The plan was simple. We would sail to Sweden, take refuge there, and wait for Estonia to be free again.

When we arrived at the dock, we couldn't find the ship we were to board. My parents looked worried. The Russian army was expected to occupy Tallinn by the next morning, and there was a desperate scramble to escape before their tanks and soldiers descended to lock us all in.

The first Soviet occupation three years earlier had provided a preview of what to expect. They had deported thousands to Siberia in freight cars, culled as enemies of the Communist Revolution. Not being politically active didn't help. They considered education and affluence crimes against the state and grounds for elimination. As dictator Stalin infamously put it: "No person, no problem."

Who was left behind or taken away was unpredictable. It was their way of inducing maximal terror and obedience. Rumor was that the Soviet officials had a quota for the number of people per week requested for slave labor camps in Siberia, and they fulfilled it without regard to age or health status as long as the head count added up.

A ship commandeered by the retreating German army to transport their wounded was preparing for departure. It was also taking along workers conscripted from an Estonian radio factory. We had mistakenly boarded their ship, thinking it an alternate one also heading for Sweden.

To our surprise, Mamma's youngest brother Paul suddenly appeared, as surprised to see us as we to see him.

"What are you doing here? I thought you were on your way to Sweden," he exclaimed.

Father was startled. "This is the only ship in the harbor that is loading up to leave. It is going to Sweden, isn't it?"

Now it was Paul's turn to look shocked.

" Oh, no. There was a ship to Sweden that left an hour ago. They were afraid to get caught here and not be able to get out, so they played safe and left early. The Germans took over this ship to take their wounded to Germany, and our whole factory was ordered to go along."

Father froze. Mother turned pale. Mamma reached out to support her, looking ashen herself as she asked her brother, "So you are going to Germany?"

"I have no choice about going," Paul said, "but they are allowing families to come along. Staying would be even worse."

He offered to talk to his boss, an engineer-type who was not a real Nazi, he said. Other workers' families were already on board, so maybe he could bring us along with him. Too late now for any more ships to sail before our capital fell, this offered the only escape.

Proceeding into the heart of the war was certainly risky, but staying was unthinkable. Father had already been taken away once by the Soviets when I was three, but the ship he was imprisoned on was sunk in the Finnish Gulf by a German bomb. He had managed to escape and swim to a small nearby island, where he hid until the advancing German army had pushed out the Russians and took its own turn occupying Estonia. He then managed to return home.

We were startled to see men start to disconnect the gangplank. Uncle Paul rushed back to tell us his boss had agreed to take us. His message was that we could stay aboard and go serve the German "Fatherland" or get off immediately. The ship was leaving.

If we got off, imprisonment or execution awaited Father, and a likely rail journey to the Siberian Gulag the rest of us. Staying aboard would at least give us a chance to aim for neutral Switzerland and ask for asylum. That could mean survival and perhaps even freedom. Besides, Mother was on the verge of giving birth, and medical personnel on the ship might help if needed. The choice was obvious.

There were several dozen other Estonians on the ship, all of us packed into a small area on the rear deck, our eyes glued to the slowly receding view of the homeland we might never see again.

As the sun dropped behind the medieval towers of Tallinn's ancient center, a rain of Russian bombs lit up the night sky with explosions and fires. Moving together as if on cue, the men stood and removed their hats, the women beside them, and sang our national anthem, cheeks streaked with tears.

I had never seen my parents weep like that. I cried with them, my heart broken too. I would try to be brave tomorrow, as Father had asked.

I spent the next few days thinking about everything we had left behind: home, my books and toys, kindergarten friends, and especially the garden where I roamed with the dogs, climbed trees, and helped the old man who worked on the vegetable patch. I had been so happy.

Now we were on a ship, crowded together with strangers and going to a place that sounded scary. It was also scary when two planes dove over our heads and dropped bombs that hit another ship behind us. We were the lucky ones the bombs missed. There were many people in the icy cold water crying for help, but our ship sailed on without stopping.

The only good thing during the days at sea was that the captain let my mother rest in his cabin every afternoon, and I could go along. We used that time to nap, and Mother didn't mind if I cried a little.

To make Father proud, I pretended to be brave in public.

Chapter 2

DESOLATION

Everything I saw through the window of the restaurant was damp and ugly, like a rain-soaked swamp in dreary gray fog. My whole body hurt with fatigue and hunger—and from something inside telling me I would never return to my beloved home.

Mother said we were now in Danzig, Germany, which meant nothing to me. Four days had passed. It felt like forever. I wanted to cry, but what had happened was too big for tears.

After we had disembarked along with Uncle Paul by blending into the group of conscripted workers, his boss told us that our family was free to go and try to get to our relatives. But that meant we were on our own, he said, and foreigners without any legal papers could get into trouble. Or we could come to the work camp with his group. That would be safer.

His giving us this choice was a surprise. During our voyage, my parents had made up a story about having German relatives near the Swiss border, and Paul had shared that information with his boss. Since

both he and my grandmother had been raised bilin-
gual by a German mother, this story was credible. Father thanked him and said we had to think about it.

We were free, but with no idea what to do next.
Hunger drove us to the only restaurant in the harbor. There was very little food available because of
the war, we were told, and what they had was tightly
rationed. All we could order was the sole item on the
menu: a watery brown soup and some dry-looking
bread.

When the waitress brought the soup, it looked so
yucky that I balked until I heard Mother's tired voice.

"Please eat your soup," she said quietly. "We may
not eat again for a long time."

I looked at her sitting next to me with red-rimmed
eyes, so uncomfortable in a hard wooden chair with
her bulging belly, and I felt like throwing up. But I
managed to force down the soup without gagging
even though it was so different from what Mamma
had cooked at home. Seeing Father's sad eyes across
the table and knowing he was counting on me to be
his brave little girl, I also forced down the stale bread.
There wasn't even any butter to make it taste better.

"How long do we have to stay here? When are we
going home?" I asked him.

"I don't know, dear. As soon as possible."

A cloud crossed his face, but his voice was steady.
My hope faded. He was a smart man who was supposed to know how to make everything okay. If he
couldn't, then things must be really bad.

"Where are we going to sleep tonight then?" It
was hard to hold back tears.

I could tell his eyes wanted to cry, too, but his voice remained steady: "I'm not sure. We'll figure something out."

That was not the answer I wanted, but sensed it was better not to talk any more. We sat in silence for a long time, each with our own thoughts. I noticed that Mamma had not said anything, just slumped in her chair looking as miserable as the weather. This was not the family I had always known.

Suddenly the front door banged open, blown by a gust of wind behind Uncle Paul. Scanning the room, he saw us, hurried over, sat down, and lowered his voice.

"Act like this is a casual conversation," he warned, "I can only stay a minute. You have to come with me right now. We are leaving and this is your last chance to join us."

My parents did their best to appear relaxed.

"Come where? And how did you get away?" Father whispered.

"The boss asked about you again, and when I told him you were trained in physics and mathematics, he said your skills would be useful. Since you are here illegally without proper documents, he says, you won't be free for long. You have nowhere to go anyway."

"We planned to travel toward Switzerland," Father said. "Wouldn't coming with you mean being confined to a camp we couldn't leave?"

"How long do you think you'd last traveling? They ask for papers everywhere. I had to get a written note just to come here and find you."

Paul's gaze bounced around nervously.

"And we have to go *now* because my allotted time is running out."

"But we would be prisoners," Mother whispered.

"Not technically prisoners, but confined behind a fence with guards, yes. Not so bad, though, they tell me. The camp is run by civilians. You would work on radio parts, and the war is going to end soon anyway. This would give you food and shelter till then. The boss likes your technical background and says he also wants to help because of the baby."

Then, barely audibly, "Hitler is obviously losing the war, but to say so is forbidden. Nobody talks about it, and all the German news sources lie."

Mother looked crestfallen, but said nothing. Father knew we had to decide quickly.

"You're right," he said, "your boss is offering at least temporary survival, and maybe we can figure out something else later. Without documents, we'd be caught on our first train ride, and for sure when and wherever the baby is born."

That thought seemed to settle it. We went with Uncle Paul.

While in transit, we were housed for several days somewhere near Danzig in bare communal rooms full of people, with straw mattresses on the floor and little else.

By that time, I had a high fever. I was miserable on a stinky mattress under a bare light bulb that hurt my eyes, lying on the floor in my clothes with blankets and coats piled on me, but still shivering.

In a thick mental fog, in and out of sleep, I was next aware of being wedged into the corner of an overcrowded train compartment with foul air and loud voices I could not understand. This was a few days later, on the way to our new camp "home."

Noting some warning signs, Mamma fretted about the possibility of Mother giving birth on the train, but help arrived unexpectedly. At a stop, two young women, wearing what looked like nurses' uniforms, boarded with some soldiers who came to check documents. When the women saw my mother's condition as well as how sick I was, they said we must get off the train immediately and go to a hospital.

After a lively discussion with the officials, they escorted Mother, Mamma, and me off the train. They even allowed Father, who was packed into the crowd outside our compartment, to come with us.

When I asked who these women were, Mother said they belonged to an organization tasked with helping women and children. When insisting on taking us off the train, the two women had promised that once the baby was born and I had recovered, they would make sure we showed up at the work camp as planned.

Father was allowed to stay with Mother on the hospital grounds through the birth, but my grandmother and I were a problem because of how sick I was.

Luckily, some nuns at a nearby convent offered to provide us both with shelter and to care for me. I panicked at the idea of being separated from both parents, but was too weak to protest. It wouldn't have made any difference anyway.

The Sisters welcomed Mamma and me warmly, though they scared me at first. Estonia was a Lutheran country, so I didn't know anything about nuns, who they were, or why they dressed so strangely. I had never seen nuns before. Their black habits made me think of witches. But they fed and cared for me so lovingly, taking such pleasure in seeing me get better, that by the time the day came for our family to leave for the work camp with my new baby sister, the nuns had become my friends.

They had been especially kind when I first came out of my feverish fog and realized that I couldn't find my beloved doll from Estonia. The nuns said they hadn't seen any doll when we arrived. Mamma thought maybe Mother had it but it turned out none of us did. It must have slipped out of my grasp on the train when I was too sick to notice.

I cried for several days while the nuns tried to console me with books and games. Then it was time to be brave again. Crying wouldn't bring my doll back, and now I would have a sister to play with.

After bidding the nuns goodbye, Mamma and I headed for the town of Schneidemühl to join my parents and the baby. I couldn't wait to see her—a playmate all my own. As an only child for six years, I had eagerly sought the company of other children, and now I would have one living with us.

I had no knowledge of newborns or birth, or any real information about Mother's big belly other than vague stories about storks and hospitals. What I pictured in my mind was someone big enough to play with.

"So small?" I exclaimed when I saw her.

What a disappointment. She was as tiny as a doll. And she mostly just nursed and slept.

Nursing was another surprise. I never knew anything about milk coming from inside a mother. In addition, though her lap was no longer full of belly, it was now occupied by the baby. There was still no room for me.

I asked when my sister could play with me, and felt even more dejected when told I had to wait a few years. She was sweet, though, so I tried to make her my living doll. But they would not allow that either. I could only hold her very briefly under close supervision, then give her right back to Mother or Mamma.

I felt completely left out. I wanted to sit on Mother's lap, too, and said so, but Mamma said I was a big girl now and didn't need to sit on laps any more. Really? That was not fair. I felt alone and lost in this strange world, everything felt wrong, and now I was expected to be a daughter who didn't need her mother any more?

Mamma couldn't stand in for Mother, the center of my world, although she tried. I sensed it was better to hide my feelings, so I kept up the brave front that made the grownups happy. But I didn't feel brave at all.

In spite of these disappointments, the two weeks in Schneidemühl had almost made me forget the war. With the battles raging far enough away, we saw no planes and few soldiers. Now, with two hospital staff seeing us off, we had to board a train again for the work camp in Märisch-Trübau, which my mother correctly guessed was in occupied Czechoslovakia.

The ride south would take at least a full day.

Chapter 3

LIFE BEHIND WIRE

The camp was on the edge of Märisch-Trübau, fenced in with a checkpoint and uniformed guards at the gate.

There were several nicer houses for the Director and his German staff, while the conscripted workers occupied rows of cement one-story buildings, with rooms along a corridor punctuated by two communal toilets and a separate washroom. These facilities were shared by all of us: individuals, couples, and a few families.

The mixture of nationalities included a handful of Estonians. As a family of five, we had one of the larger rooms to ourselves, with just enough space for two bunk beds, one along each of two walls, a small coal stove for heat and cooking, a few pots and kitchen tools, and a wooden table with four hard chairs.

The buildings must have been newly constructed, because the musty smell of wet plaster remained strong as long as we were there. With the coming of winter, the buildings never fully dried.

Baby slept next to Mother's bed in a nice but worn carriage given to us at the birthing hospital. I slept on one of the top bunks, Father on the other, with Mother below him and Mamma below me. I didn't mind the up-and-down climb, because it provided a kind of private space up there, where I read anything I could find and wrote some sad poetry that made me feel better and surprised my father. I wasn't sure why.

I was required to go to school in the village outside the fence, even though I didn't speak German except for a few words and phrases, like please, thank you, yes, no, and "I don't understand," which I said a lot. Either Mother or Mamma walked me there and back. Father was always at work and could not leave the camp at all.

I soon understood some German, starting with "damned foreigner," and could not wait for dismissal time. Because I was a whiz at math, the teachers realized I was smart and were nicer to me than to several other foreigners. Still, I didn't feel safe there and it was obvious that none of the children liked me.

After I could communicate a bit, a girl in my class asked if I wanted to play dolls with her at her house. She was the first one who was friendly toward me, so I was happy to say yes. She turned out to be the daughter of the camp Director. She came with her mother to pick me up and take me to their house.

It seemed like forever since I had been in a real home, playing with real toys. It was fun but also a painful reminder of my own losses. Though I only went to her house a few times, we hung out more in school after that.

Because she was the Director's daughter, her being friendly to me also led to better treatment by the other children, who stopped calling me names. Now they actually seemed glad to include me in their recess games. Perhaps they had thought they were not supposed to like me, but when someone in authority became my friend, they could also.

I started to feel better about the camp after that, except for how cold it was, especially when we played in the snow without boots or enough warm clothing.

We were all in the same boat, though, so we adapted and ran around more to keep warm. There was nowhere else to play. The outdoors was the only place with enough room for more than two or three of us to play together at the same time.

In the evening our family stayed close to the stove in our room, reading and telling stories. I never heard any conversation about Germany or world events even though I would have liked to know more.

When I asked, Father said that the less I knew beyond our ordinary daily activities the better. He told me not to worry. They would make sure I was safe. But I could tell he was worried himself. Teachers often asked students about their home activities.

I had already decided it was better not to ask certain questions. Despite what I heard in school, I harbored the feeling that Hitler was a very bad man, and when I said so to my parents at home, they were strangely quiet and didn't respond. I thought they looked uneasy, so I put that first on my list of what not to talk about even to them, and certainly not to anyone else. There was something vaguely ominous in the air whenever the *Führer* was mentioned, even in school.

I did ask them why we always had to raise our arm and say "I won't say it" whenever a teacher entered the classroom. They looked puzzled, then caught on and laughed. *Ei ütle* when mumbled rapidly in Estonian sounded a bit like *heil Hitler*.

"That's fine," said Father with a smile. "Customs here are different. Keep saying it, but do it softly because if you say it louder the teachers will try to correct you. It's better to say it quickly and quietly so they won't notice."

I did as I was told, still mystified by this strange custom.

My parents had packed a few Estonian children's books, which I read cover to cover many times. My favorite was *Sellid*—Rascals—about three mischievous kittens. The other, *Tasuja*, The Avenger, meant for older kids, told about a young Estonian hero who led a revolt against a particularly evil baron several centuries earlier, when everyone was suffering at the hands of German conquerors. That one was a challenge, but, lacking other books, it improved my reading skills in short order as I read it over and over.

At the same time, I was a reluctant student of German. Because I hated not knowing what people around me were saying, I learned in spite of myself, but I still resented being forced to learn their language. I planned to forget it as soon as I could.

As several months went by, my parents looked more and more worried. They often talked together very quietly out of my earshot, and my attempts to eavesdrop failed to yield any information. The war still raged on, though we had no idea what was really happening. If my parents knew, they kept it to themselves.

All we heard was endless Nazi propaganda about the glorious exploits of German troops fighting for the Fatherland.

Uncle Paul had said Germany was losing, which meant that the Russians were probably getting closer. If we stayed trapped where we were, all our efforts to save ourselves would have been in vain. We might still be taken to Siberia.

Meanwhile, I was getting more used to camp life, and developed several friends.

A ten-year-old Estonian boy taught me to play checkers. It was our only board game, and we played often. Soon I started winning, and he would throw down his pieces and walk out the door, slamming it hard. Mother said she could tell when I had won because the room would shake. He would return in a little while, and the game would resume. But I especially liked to play with him because we could speak Estonian.

At school, I was beginning to understand more German, so that part of my life was also getting better. I had food, our room, other children to play with, and my parents nearby.

Not having toys forced us to create things to do and games to play on our own. We relied on reading, make-believe, fabricated games, and making toys from whatever objects we could find lying around.

The checkers battles were fought on a cardboard square with hand-drawn boxes, and different-colored stones as the pieces.

I missed my home terribly, but secretly nurtured the idea that we would go back there when the war was over, which would be soon. In the meantime, things were not so bad. I didn't mind at all that the whole family had to share a room. It felt cozy and secure. I felt myself slowly settling into our fenced-in life.

To my surprise, I soon found out my parents were planning a trip. Could we actually do that? Since Easter was approaching, Father had asked the Director if the family could get a holiday traveling pass for a week, to visit our "German relatives" near Switzerland. That sounded like fun. I had never heard anything about these relatives.

Extracting a promise that we would return right after Easter, the Director issued the traveling papers, perhaps doubting our story but having no quick way to check. Reliable communication systems had all broken down. His job, however, did not require preventing women and children from spending Easter with their relatives, and Mamma's fluency in German made our having such relatives credible.

We packed two suitcases for our "vacation" trip, leaving the rest of our possessions behind since we were supposedly coming back. When it was time to leave, I was so happy to see that Father was coming to the station with us, though I wondered why a uniformed guard with a gun came with hum.

I soon found out. When Father told Mother to give his regards to "Cousin Ursula" I realized with a shock that he was staying behind.

I had been so pleased and surprised to think that the permission included our whole family, but now realized with a lump in my throat why the guard was there: to make sure Father would go back. He had never been allowed to leave the camp before, so his being allowed to come to the station at all was a stretch of the rules—a gift from the camp director.

I held back tears when he kissed my forehead and wished me a good trip.

"Why can't you come with us?" I wailed in Estonian, "We need you."

His eyes welled up but he caught himself, then said cheerfully in German so that the guard could hear: "I have to work, but you all have a nice Easter and decorate a few eggs for me. I'll be waiting to see you again."

His cheerful tone felt phony and I wasn't sure exactly what he said, but the guard was watching so I forced a smile.

He said goodbye to Mother last, and they hugged in a way I had not seen before. They held each other as though they wanted to melt into one person. Though both were smiling, their eyes were crying even without tears.

Then Mother turned and briskly walked us all up the steps into the train without looking at him again. We found seats and I pressed my nose to the window for another look. Father was walking away with the guard, but turned around briefly and looked in our direction one more time before they disappeared around a corner.

I was no longer excited about going on a trip and meeting new relatives. The knot in my stomach told me something very bad was happening that I didn't understand, and I wanted us to stay. But the train was already moving.

Chapter 4

JOURNEY TO NOWHERE

The train was crowded, with many languages spoken around us that I couldn't understand. We were not the only ones escaping westward.

Many of the passengers were German, and they told us the war was almost over, lacking only the formality of final surrender. The Allies had won. No one knew for sure where Hitler was or whether he was still alive, but they did know the Russian front was advancing, and getting close.

The war's end was good news, but it didn't change our situation, except that now information was passed along easily. To tell whether something was true or just a rumor was the real challenge. There was no true German government anymore and nothing had replaced it, so everything was in chaos, including news media.

Like us, the East Germans and other Eastern Europeans on the train were trying to escape the Russians. All fled to seek safety with the Western Allies, who were said to be more humane. The Russian army was

seen as a murderous wave of brutality rolling westward, raping and looting as they came.

Everyone wanted to be with the Americans, but
would settle for the British or the French. Unless
they were German. They feared the French almost
as much as the Russians. When I asked why, I was
told that the Germans had been very cruel when they
had occupied France earlier during the war and they
were now afraid the French would retaliate.

We struck up a conversation with another Estonian family of women and children, and decided to
travel together as far as we could. They had no specific destination either. One of the women had a husband who, like Father, had helped them escape but
could not join them. A second woman, her sister, had
lost her husband to the war, and between the two of
them they had three small children. Their mother
was also with them, so we now became a traveling
group of ten: two grandmothers, three mothers, and
five children ranging from my infant sister to my ripe
old age of six.

That was a big group to be traveling together, but
Mother was always ready to help where needed. She
and Mamma spoke German, which would be useful to
the whole group, and perhaps traveling together with
other Estonians would make the children feel safer.

I wasn't sure about that, since I noticed very
quickly that the needs of the smaller children always
seemed to trump mine. But it was probably true for
them.

The train crawled along, stopping often, its hyp-
notic chug-chug and rattles punctuated by sounds of

gunfire and bomb explosions at various distances, though not right near the train. There was sporadic fighting along the way, and the train stopped to wait it out when the sounds came too close. Not a good place to be, but there was no other transportation in the direction we needed to go, so we tried to get some sleep.

So far, we had made it to one major city someone said was Prague, and left again after a brief stop, having been warned that the Russians would probably overrun the city within twenty-four to forty-eight hours. But if all went well, we would be far ahead of them by the following morning.

All did not go well. We were over halfway to our next destination where we planned to find another train going farther west, when suddenly the train stopped and reversed direction. It did not stop again until we were back to the city we had just left, the one expected to be under Russian control within a day.

This was devastating. When asked, the conductor said they had received orders to return to the station we had originally departed from, now under Soviet control. We would continue back in that direction within an hour. Meanwhile, if we wanted to look for some food at the station, we should hurry.

Food was the least of our problems. People were crying, cursing, some screaming out loud. Mother was thinking of a way to get off the train and continue on foot—but how fast and how far could our group walk with so many small children? Thinking we could outpace the Russian army was a pipedream. Yet there was no other alternative.

A stranger unexpectedly intervened. We had met him by chance shortly after we first boarded the train.

While looking for a bathroom we could use and a spot where she might have some privacy for nursing the baby, Mother took both of us to the train car next to ours. It was almost empty, with a stack of boxes and only a few people sitting at the other end. The contrast to the rest of the train, with every car packed to the ceiling with people and luggage, seemed odd, but there was a bathroom to our left.

As we approached it, a woman—one of a group of four sitting at the other end of the car—shouted at us that this was their private car and we should find another bathroom. I really had to go, so Mother asked if we could use it just this once, and a man, in a gentler voice, said, "Of course."

The woman glared at him, but he seemed not to notice.

There must have been something about us that caught his interest, because he came over and asked where we were going at a time like that with such a little baby. When Mother explained our situation, he invited us to use the empty end of the car whenever we needed some privacy or rest. The invitation did not include our fellow travelers, so we only spent time there when Mother needed to feed or change the baby.

Gradually there was more conversation, and soon the initially hostile wife became friendlier and even invited Mamma to join us.

The husband turned out to be the owner of a well-known German champagne company, and he had bought his way to his spacious accommodations with bottles of champagne. Money was almost useless at this stage of societal collapse, he said, but liquor was in great demand. Just one bottle of champagne could buy a lot, and he had a stack of full boxes with him.

Motivated like us to get away from the Russian front, when the shock of our order to return came he used his liquid currency as a bribe to get his car hooked onto a train that went in the direction we had been headed. It would take a different route, but would still easily outpace the Russian army and get closer to the Allies.

In a burst of generosity, he invited us to bring our luggage and join his family in the about-to-be-rerouted car. Mother asked if she could also bring our companions, since we had agreed to travel together. He looked uncertain but not unwilling. He would have to ask his wife, he said.

We went back to our own car and waited.

He returned quickly and pulled Mother aside. His wife refused to take the others, but was quite willing to take just our family.

Mother's face went pale. This was a miraculous opportunity for us, but would leave the others in grave danger. She knew the dire prospects if we did not take advantage of this invitation, but it would be even worse for our companions if we left them. If she accepted, she would always know that she had abandoned three women and three little children to a life-threatening situation.

There was an awkward silence.

"I can't leave them to the Gulag. I couldn't live with myself," she finally said, eyes overflowing, "But thank you. Your invitation is so kind."

The man looked at her in disbelief.

"Do you know what that means for your own family?"

Her desolate but resigned face told him more eloquently than words, and he saw that her decision was final. Dumbfounded, he turned without further comment and went back to his private car.

I could sense Mother's pain even through my own fear. She saw and caressed my cheek.

"I know, my love. But we can't leave them to the Russians."

Then, just before his car was about to be disconnected from our train, he rushed back and told us all to come quickly and bring our bags, stipulating that we, and especially the rest of our group, were to stay at the other end of the car and not intrude in any way upon his family. He had overruled his wife's objection, but promised her that "these people" would not bother her.

We didn't. We all behaved and even charmed him, if not his wife. Mother asked me to not say anything to our companions about her conversation with the nice man. All they knew was that they were suddenly invited to the next car, which would take us all toward safety.

We spent many hours in the back of that car, and had the opportunity to sleep a little despite the now farther-away sounds of intermittent bombings. These were said to be American planes bombing Germany into final submission.

What puzzled me was why, if Americans were the people we were trying to get to for help, were they dropping bombs that destroyed buildings and killed people not far from us? They could easily hit us, too. And why did people like the nice man with the champagne bottles want to run away from their own country to the ones who were bombing it?

The world made less and less sense to me as we went along, and since no one had any good answers, even now that I sensed it was safe to ask questions, I figured I would simply follow Mother's lead and speak as little as possible. Maybe it would all make sense when I grew up. In the meantime, we were going to see these relatives in Switzerland I never knew we had, and that at least sounded pleasant.

And—a cheerful thought—maybe Father could finally join us there now that the war was almost over.

Chapter 5

Endless Walk

We chugged along slowly for a very long time. I slept through most of it, but when they woke me up we had to get off because the tracks ahead had been wiped out by a bomb. The train was not going any farther.

Our benefactor decided to use his remaining champagne to hire a car for his family. He apologized for having to leave us, but gave us several bottles to use for barter and, deflecting our expressions of gratitude, wished us safe arrival in the American Zone. He looked genuinely sad that he couldn't take us with him.

Now our feet became our sole means of travel, and with our multigenerational group it was slow going. At least the Russian front was now farther behind us. This train ride had bought us time. We picked up our belongings and walked out of the station.

With no idea where we were or the current political situation there, we decided to stay put for a day or two to regroup, but within twenty-four hours we were on the road. To make that possible, Mother had traded one of our bottles of champagne for a wooden wagon to hold our luggage and to carry the smaller children when they were too tired.to walk The other women took turns pulling the wagon while Mother pushed the baby carriage.

She quickly developed a standard approach to finding shelter when we entered a new town. Leaving us all somewhere as inconspicuous as possible, she went to seek out the mayor or whoever was in charge of the town at the time. Since we were in the gap between the advancing Russians and the retreating Americans, most of these places were still under local German control.

There were usually lines of petitioners waiting to see these officials, but somehow Mother always managed to get an audience.

There was something about her that seemed to elicit a helpful response. She almost always returned with permission to occupy whatever refugee housing was available or, if none, she was directed to some kind of private lodging. We had to pay for those, so the pieces of jewelry and silver Mother had stashed in her purse when we left Estonia became our currency.

Sometimes nothing worked out and we spent the night outdoors. Even so, Mother managed to get permission from the authorities for us to be out after curfew. Although the war was clearly over, most of the towns remaining under German jurisdiction still adhered to curfews and other wartime regulations, whether it made sense or not.

Thank God it was spring. Sheltered by bushes and trees, sleeping outdoors was not so bad. I liked it better than some of the crumbling buildings we'd slept in.

The next weeks of walking on foot through Germany, trying to reach the Americans and stay ahead of the Russians, were a blur of nameless towns. I was hungry most of the time. We ate sporadically and slept where we could, mostly outdoors in partly bombed-out buildings and sometimes in designated buildings uninhabited because of bomb damage where refugees could seek shelter. This required permission from whoever was in charge of the civil structures still standing.

Sometimes these places had mattresses on the floor, usually not clean but softer than a bare floor. Those were the best, because there was often also a functioning toilet or washroom nearby. And once in a while, we were able to bargain for a room in a real house.

Early on in our endless walk, we found a room upstairs in a private house that was quite nice. The people in that town seemed to be mostly Czech, speaking a language I did not understand at all, but they were quite friendly to us. Something happened there that etched a haunting image into my mind.

One day, as Mother and I walked into the paved courtyard in front of a low U-shaped building where we were renting a room overnight, we saw Mamma hanging on to a broomstick stretched across a hole in the asphalt, surrounded by a group of agitated

people. I couldn't understand what they were saying, but the air smelled terrible.

I quickly realized that she had fallen into the hole
the smell was coming from.

Mother hastily assured me that Mamma was all
right and the people around her would pull her out.
Then she quickly hustled me indoors into our room
where the baby was sleeping. She told me to stay
there and look after her while she herself ran back
out.

Unknown to us, there was a cesspool under part
of the courtyard, covered by wood boards and then
paved over. A part had given way when Mamma
walked over it, and she fell into the hole, unable to
pull herself out because the hole was too deep. Some
of the neighbors had heard her call for help and come
to her rescue, placing a broomstick across the opening that was supported by intact asphalt on both
sides.

She hung on for dear life while they debated
how to hoist her out. There was a lot of talking back
and forth. It was unclear how solid the asphalt that
seemed intact really was, and no one wanted to fall
in with her. If their weight made more of the surface
collapse, the broomstick would drop into the cesspool and Mamma could drown.

I was both revolted and scared, but had to stay
away until it was over. I tried to see as much as I
could through the window without Mother realizing
I was looking, but too many people were in the way.

They did manage to get her out, and she got
cleaned up somehow, somewhere. Later, when I

next saw her, she acted perfectly normal, as though nothing had happened. I couldn't imagine what this experience must have felt like, and shuddered every time I thought of it. Imagine if she'd had no help and drowned.

The people who saved her had really been nice, like the champagne man on the train. I was impressed that they had helped us when they didn't have to, while others we met while walking had cursed us as damn foreigners.

I had nightmares about this incident despite Mamma's assurances that everything was fine and I needn't worry about her.

I really wanted to know more details about how the rescue was carried out, but nothing more was forthcoming. The grownups didn't talk about it, at least with me in earshot, so all I was left with was the image of her in that stinky hole, desperately hanging on to a broomstick.

Another image that wouldn't leave my mind was from a railroad station around this same time. We walked past a string of boxcars filled with wounded soldiers, with the doors open for fresh air. They were lying on stretchers or sitting, some smoking, with bloody bandages, missing limbs, ragged uniforms, and grizzled faces. Their uniforms looked German, but more like rags. The air smelled so awful that I gagged.

It was the first time I had seen this part of war close up, and it shocked me. Why do people do that to each other, I wondered, when the ones who make war suffer from it themselves?

The walking went on endlessly—grim, gritty, in-cessant walking. All day, every day, on slushy coun-try roads and roads with traffic, across fields and through the woods. Put one foot in front of the other, ignore being tired because we can't stop no matter what, and don't complain that the younger children get to take turns riding on top of the luggage in the wagon. I was the big girl who had to keep up with the adults, even though my feet hurt, my shoes were falling apart, and I was often so tired I was afraid I would keel over onto the muddy road.

Sometimes I felt like really doing that—just let-ting go and collapsing on the road. I wondered what it would be like to die right there. Would angels come and take me to wherever Heaven was? I knew no one else could pick me up and carry me.

The adults were not being cruel. I was too heavy for any of them to carry even if they wanted to, and my weight would also make the wagon's load too heavy for them to pull. None of them was very strong.

Despite these thoughts, I braved on like the troup-er my father had asked me to be. I couldn't let him down, even though I was getting increasingly upset that he had sent us off into this horrible situation and wasn't there to protect us.

Wasn't that what he was supposed to do? I thought fathers were all-powerful and could do pret-ty much what they wanted, so I now questioned his statement that he couldn't come with us. If he really, really wanted to, he surely would have found a way. I missed him so much, but now I was angry, too, and these mixed feelings confused me.

Life felt very complicated, and trying to figure it out made my head hurt. It was better not to think about it at all. Just keep on walking.

Chapter 6

EPIPHANY

At one point, we stopped in a sizable town longer than usual because everyone was ready to drop from exhaustion, and we were lucky to be housed in a damaged schoolhouse that was in pretty good shape.

It was relatively comfortable, a good place to rest and regroup. We were a fairly safe distance ahead of the Russian front now, and it was rumored that their advance might stop where they were. We sure hoped so. We shared a classroom with about thirty other people, most speaking languages I did not understand.

Our family terrain consisted of four mattresses lined up on the floor along one wall, happily near a window through which we could see a tree. There was hardly any uncovered space, so lying down and sitting were the only indoor options. The alternative was the outdoors, which I chose as often and for as long as I could.

All of the refugees were warned to stay away from a dreary gray stone building across the street, but curiosity led several of us kids to explore anyway.

Through some opaque basement windows with bars, we heard people moaning and occasional muted screams, as though the screamer were too tired to produce more sound, and then dull impact thuds of something hard hitting something softer—ugly sounds that made my skin crawl. I realized someone was being beaten.

Who was doing this? To whom? And why? My listening in on adult conversations had confirmed that the building was being used as a prison, but whose? The element of danger upped the ante on the kids' ongoing "I dare you" game.

The fear of getting caught sneaking across the street to peek into the building made it all the more exciting. Speaking a cacophony of mutually incomprehensible words but somehow bonded by a need to play that transcended language, we ignored the warning until several of us got caught. A menacing-looking guard told us, according to an older boy who spoke German, that if he caught us there again, he would lock us up too.

That gave us pause for a while, but with no toys and nowhere else to play, the dare game resumed once our fear subsided.

I did not like this game, but played along enough to avoid exclusion from the only group of playmates available. It didn't feel right to sneak over there and listen to the sounds of other people's pain, and it didn't feel like a game.

I much preferred to go to a church down the street and stand by the door, especially when the candles on the altar were lit and the choir was singing—although this, too, was beyond designated bounds. Children were supposed to stay in and around our shelter.

I had no idea whether the church was Protestant or Catholic, and didn't care. It comforted me and, though I dared not fully enter when it was in use, I loved standing by the door and listening to the singing. For a little while, I could imagine a world where angels were possible and life felt good. It also reminded me of home somehow.

One day, as I started back toward the schoolhouse, I stopped short, as if frozen in place.

I could still hear the church choir singing its unearthly melodies, their voices wafting toward heaven through the intricate vaulted ceiling, while from the other side of the square, like a direct punch to the gut, I heard again those ugly thuds of something forcefully smashing into human flesh. This time the screams were piercingly loud enough to drown out the choir and puncture the flow of melody emanating from inside the church.

I stared at the building the screams were coming from. This sudden collision of the angelic and the infernal flooded me with the excruciating reality of where I was—in a country called Deutschland, far from my lost home, in a small nameless city I knew not where, the schoolhouse the last in a succession of temporary makeshift shelters, and something terrible going on directly across the street. And with an uncertain future I did not want to think about—if we *had* a future.

As I took in the sounds of heavenly music on one side and on the other, screams of pain inflicted by humans on other humans, I knew with total wordless clarity that this was insane.

It was a moment of timeless, stunned indignation. How could the people on my left keep singing as though everything were fine, while on my right others were torturing their fellow human beings? How could this be? It was so wrong. Surely the loving God I had been told about never meant this.

The whole world—life—suddenly made no sense. Who was responsible? Who could set it right?

After this, I started thinking about life and death, good and bad, and why people behaved as they did. If children from different countries without a common language could play together and be friends, why couldn't grownups? Weren't they supposed to be smarter than we?

I needed some answers. Even if I had to keep on walking until we were safe, I would figure it out someday. There was something terribly wrong in this world, and when I grew up I would have to understand it and make it better.

After we left that town, there were also some bright moments. Spring flowers were in bloom, and we were traveling through a beautiful part of southern Germany where, on clear days, we could see the snow-clad Alps in the distance.

That thrilled me. I had never seen mountains like that before, and most of our refugee days had been spent cooped up in unpleasant places. If not for fatigue and ever-present hunger, being outdoors in the heady air of springtime in this glorious landscape could have been fun.

We walked again for several full days, trying to get to a town we heard had been occupied by the American army. If everyone held up and no one got sick or injured, Mother thought we could get there in two or three more days.

For me, more days felt daunting. I really wanted to stop—anywhere! My city shoes, never intended for this kind of workout but the only ones I had, were starting to seriously hurt my feet. My knees hurt too. So did my whole body. The grey morning mist around us matched my mood perfectly. But braving on had become a habit by now.

We were walking along a road bordered on both sides by a row of chestnut trees standing like green guards at attention as we passed. I glanced down the road ahead and, as if in response, the sky suddenly cleared above a low-hanging cloudbank, revealing bright sunshine on a snow-clad mountain peak.

It took my breath away. Framed by the trees on both sides of the road, with a burst of sunrays turning the snow into a sparkling blanket capping the summit, what I saw looked like a golden island in the sky beckoning me onward. Although it looked like a postcard, this was real, and straight ahead in the direction we were walking.

I felt a surge of hope. Maybe God was telling us that everything really will be all right.

Walking became easier after that. When I felt tired or hungry, when my feet hurt, when I missed Father or thought of the home I had lost, I would

picture that luminous mountain and feel better. It
even seemed to me that Mother and the others were
a little happier—or maybe it was just that I was seeing them through happier eyes.

Still, it took longer than Mother expected for us
to reach the next town. We didn't see them at first,
but were told that Americans actually were in charge
there,

Suddenly it felt as though a heavy burden had
been lifted. We all grinned at each other, too tired
to express our excitement. We needed to see the local mayor about housing, but it could wait until next
morning. Meanwhile, we had a happy evening and a
welcome rest among freshly green bushes. We slept
better that night than we had in a long time, knowing
that we were finally safe.

Chapter 7

FATEFUL ENCOUNTER

The next morning, Mamma set out to look for food. Through our whole trek, largely on rural roads, she had always been busy searching for food. She was not too proud to go begging in order to feed us.

Some of the local farmers along the way were hostile, but many had shared what they could when they heard it was for mothers in distress and their hungry children. We often got potatoes they had intended to feed their pigs, coarse country bread, sometimes even an egg or two and a little milk for the children. Those were the really good days.

The best nourished of us all was my sister, because miraculously Mother still had ample breast milk. Since there were ten of us, there was not much food for any one person, but thanks to Mamma we were never starving. She had learned great practical skills in her youth, a time when boys were educated in school and girls were taught domestic skills at home. She could create a meal out of practically nothing, and often did.

I had no idea how she managed to cook the potatoes and eggs the farmers gave us, make sure the baby's diapers were clean and our clothes presentable, and make sure we were as comfortable as possible when sleeping outdoors. She somehow made it look easy, and we took her everyday magic for granted.

The baby carriage had developed a wobbly wheel, so Mother decided to go to town and look for someone to fix it. With Mamma off on her daily mission, and our companions staying put to look after our belongings, Mother and I walked to town with the baby, hoping to get the carriage fixed. It was a sunny day and the warm rays felt so good now that we could relax.

Barely had we approached the central square when an American army truck drove up and stopped. Three armed soldiers got out. Their apparent leader, whom the other two addressed as Sarge and who looked older, strode up to Mother and asked for documents. She was happy to oblige, and told him she could speak some English. He walked to the driver, who handed him a notebook with pieces of loose paper inside. He scanned one and turned back toward us.

"Oh, I see you're from Estonia," he said cheerfully. "We have orders to take you to our Russian allies. They will take you back to your homeland."

His tone suggested that this should make us happy.

Mother's face drained of all color.

"We have no homeland now," she tried to explain, "the Russians took it over and they kill people like us, or send them to Siberia to die. And their troops rape women, even very young girls. We have seen what they're like. If we go back we will die. Please let us go to our relatives in Switzerland."

"You're wrong," countered Sarge. "They're our allies so they're not as bad as you say. You've heard too much German propaganda."

"Yes, they are as bad as I say. I know what will happen."

"We have to send you back, so let's get on with it. We'll help you with the carriage." He sounded impatient, expecting her to obey.

The baby was quiet but awake in her low-slung, wobbly carriage, her little blonde head sticking out from beneath a smudged blanket frayed at the edges. Mother took a protective step toward her, then said quietly,

"No, I will *not* get on that truck."

She said it with no drama, no sign of emotion, simply stating what was so. I stared at my gentle, soft-spoken mother in astonishment, too scared to move or make a sound. I bit into my coat collar instead.

Her whole being became very still—an extreme stillness beyond fear and struggle, or even ordinary emotion. Her big sea-green eyes, deep and calm, exuded total certainty. In spite of her well-tailored beige suit having streaks of dirt on the back, her worn dust-covered shoes, and a failed effort to fully tame her hair, her rumpled appearance did not detract from her regal presence, but somehow enhanced it instead. I could feel no fear in her.

Sarge's face flushed bright red. He pulled out his revolver, pointed it at her chest, and barked:

"You and your children *will* get on that truck!"

His voice betrayed a tremor, as though trying to muster as much authority as he could in the face of her unwavering gaze.

Her stillness only deepened, as though rooting her into the earth where she stood. One of the two soldiers flanking Sarge now followed Sarge's example and aimed the barrel of his rifle at Mother, looking very nervous. The driver craned his neck from the truck to see what was going on.

Mother didn't move or flinch in the face of the guns. The younger soldiers gawked helplessly, their gazes bouncing between her and their superior. Sarge pointed at the carriage and waved his hand. The two soldiers understood and lifted the carriage onto the truck. Sensing her increased distance from her mother, the baby began to whimper. Sarge glared at Mother.

"*Now* will you get on that truck?"

"No. You will have to shoot me. I prefer to die here," she said quietly.

There was no doubt she meant it. I bit even harder into my coat collar to keep from screaming. How could this be? These were the people who were supposed to save us. We had suffered so much to get to them.

Except for Sarge, they looked like teenage boys playing war. But this was real—both the guns and the war that was finally ending. It was Germany in the spring of 1945, and the Western Allies were withdrawing from East Germany as they handed it over to the Russians, who demanded "repatriation" of all refugees from the countries they had conquered. The

Allies complied. Most of the "repatriates" were never heard from again.

The soldiers looked even more nervous. I noticed beads of perspiration on Sarge's temple, in spite of the brisk cold of this early spring morning.

Suddenly, I had an astonishing realization. The men with the guns were more afraid of my mother than she of them. I stared at her and Sarge in disbelief. I didn't realize that these American boys had come there to fight a just war against Nazis, not to shoot defenseless women and children, and certainly not to hurt babies. They could easily have picked Mother up, of course, and forced her onto the truck, but somehow they seemed paralyzed, reluctant to touch her or even approach.

Sarge took a tentative step forward and aimed his gun directly at her heart. The other two shifted awkwardly from one foot to the other.

Mother held her ground. I still sensed no fear in her, and realized she was now my only home and security, the only safe haven in an incomprehensible and violent world. Though oddly reassured by her calm, my eyes were still glued to the guns, and I couldn't help gnawing my collar.

No more words were exchanged. I held my breath. The atmosphere felt like a thunderstorm brewing, with lightning about to strike.

Then, abruptly, as though cutting an invisible cord stretched to its limit, Sarge lowered his gun and snapped: "Take that carriage off the truck."

The two soldiers hastened to comply, visibly relieved.

"And you," Sarge shouted, waving his trembling index finger at Mother, "take your children and get the hell outta here! And don't ever let me see your face again."

"Thank you," Mother whispered, as she scooped her children to her like a mother hen and rushed down the street toward the next uncertainty. The broken wheel wobbled, and she almost had to carry the unbalanced carriage to keep it upright. I ran alongside hanging on to her skirt, wishing for a free hand for me to hold.

"What're you staring at?" we heard Sarge growl at the gawking truck driver, who had been taking all this in.

"Come on! Let's get a move-on!"

We got away as fast as we could. Now that we knew what was afoot, we obviously had to be careful to stay as invisible as possible to avoid running into any more American soldiers.

We were shocked to suddenly find ourselves hiding from the very people we had been looking to for safety. But if we could manage to fade into the woodwork until things settled down and they had finished their "repatriation" sweep, we would at least be in the American-occupied zone.

Chapter 8

INTO THE WOODS

Two days later, we heard that the Americans were gone. They had left during the night. The Allies were pulling back to let the advancing Soviet troops occupy the areas that were to become the Russian Zone.

The jaws of the Gulag were at our heels again. Having learned the hard way what a Russian occupation was like, the grown-ups were speechless. The Western Allies had already conquered these areas. Were they really handing them over to the Russians? Had they lost their minds?

After more than three months of grueling effort and finally thinking we were safe, this was a crushing blow. That same day we started walking again, once more in the no-man's-land between the advancing Soviet army and the now retreating Americans.

There were now even more refugees, especially Germans, who voted their preference for an American occupation with their feet, or whatever vehicles were available.

This trek dragged on for days until we finally heard that the zone boundary had been set several kilometers ahead, in the middle of a rural, largely forested area beyond a small village, with only one paved road going from one side of the border to the other. We hastened to get to the village before nightfall, hoping to finally arrive decisively in the now official "American Zone."

The road was clogged with people and their vehicles, though most of us were on foot. Getting closer to the checkpoint, we noticed a number of people walking back in the direction we had come from. They looked depressed and moved slowly, as though walking to their doom. A bad omen.

We soon discovered that the road had just been closed at the border, and not one more person would be allowed to cross the newly established zone boundary.

A sizeable contingent of American soldiers was in charge of enforcement, pending the arrival of Russian troops who would then take over. We were told that the person in charge of announcing this in several languages had emphasized that border enforcement would be strict and systematic. If people attempted to cross, they would be risking their lives.

This devastating news explained the funereal procession of the rejected, heading back to wherever they had come from—a final blow after the huge effort of getting so close to what they thought would be safety. Deliverance had seemed so near—and was now out of reach.

Was this the end then? Not for Mother. For her, no misfortune was final. While she still had breath and a capacity to act, she would not despair.

"We'll find a way," was all she said.

After we learned this dreadful news, we veered off the road onto a narrow unpaved path at the edge of the village, next to fields and a farmhouse with adjacent barn. A small sign above the farmhouse door indicated it was a *Gasthaus* (inn). From where we were, the path wound slightly uphill toward it.

Mother led us to the field across from the house to rest by some haystacks, trying to be as inconspicuous as possible. We needed the rest, and she needed a place to sit and feed the baby. I lay down on the hay, which felt soft and welcoming, though I knew I couldn't go to sleep because we'd have to forge on. Where? I had no idea.

Just when everyone had begun to relax, we spotted a man hurrying in our direction. We hadn't seen him coming until he was almost upon us. He demanded to know who we were and what we were doing on his property. He didn't look friendly.

Mother calmly told him our story, how tired we were, and how devastated about the border closing. She explained why our history with the Russians made our getting into the American Zone a life-or-death issue. We were also exhausted from the push to get to the border before nightfall, and it was already dusk.

"Could we please rest here till morning?" she asked. "We are all exhausted, especially the children, and the long journey back will be so much harder than coming here, where we thought we'd be safe."

He looked more sympathetic now, smiling at the baby and us kids.

"Very well, you can rest till morning," he said, "but you have to leave early, before sunrise, because soldiers sometimes come here for breakfast. We're not allowed to talk with refugees other than to sell them food for traveling. They are not allowed to stay at the inn."

He surely guessed what Mother was contemplating when she asked:

"By the way, is there any other road or out-of-the-way path that might bypass the roadblocks and soldiers guarding the border?"

He said no, glancing pointedly at the forest above his house.

"No way at all," he repeated with emphasis, looking intently toward the forest as he spoke.

Mother seemed to understand what he said, but not be too upset about it. I wondered why. He was saying there was no hope.

"I think it would be better if you slept in the barn where you would have privacy," he added, "but only if you can manage to not be either seen or heard no matter what happens. Can you guarantee that, with all the children and a baby? Soldiers will be coming here at night to drink, and if they catch you I'll be in trouble."

Mother assured him we could do that, and thanked him. She tried to hold back tears as he led us to the barn in a circuitous path around the back of the building.

His eyes were very soft when he shook her hand and wished us all good luck on our "return trip," then closed the barn door behind him and left.

Immensely grateful, we settled down at the back of the barn, behind stacks of hay so we could not be seen from the area near the door in case someone came in to get something. There were no animals there, most likely commandeered for the war effort long ago to feed the German army. The hay that sheltered us had probably been intended for them, but now provided some softness for our tired bodies.

The newly improvised plan was for the children to get several hours of sleep, and then, once the bar was closed and the resident family had retired for the night, we would quietly set out to cross the border through the forest. The adults would take turns napping while one kept watch.

Suddenly the barn door opened and we heard two male voices. Having been warned, we assumed they were members of the border patrol.

Each adult automatically tasked herself with holding one child to comfort and keep quiet. Mother understood enough English to recognize them as either American or British, and their conversation had more to do with drinking and women than their military duties, so they were not looking for us, simply having a smoke and what they meant to be a private conversation.

We could hardly breathe. The biggest worry was the baby, but she was asleep at the breast and miraculously, as the conversation dragged on, not one adult or child made a sound that could have betrayed our presence.

After the soldiers left, we decided to head for the forest as soon as it was dark enough to sneak out without being seen. We would go in pairs, one adult and child at a time, and regroup right beyond the first cluster of trees visible from the barn doorway, staying low and dodging for cover whenever available. The smallest children were asleep, and were to be carried.

I went last with Mother and the baby in her carriage. I wasn't going to let her out of my sight. We were potentially the most easily visible group because of the bulk and light color of the carriage. The dark blanket covering it did not reach all the way.

My sister turned out to be quite a sleeper. She didn't cry or make any sound while her carriage was being pushed over bumpy ground for many hours through the night.

Not knowing where the border was, we simply walked in the direction the Americans seemed to be, and knew we were right when, around midnight, they began sporadic rounds of firing randomly into the forest, in our direction.

They were obviously not aiming specifically at us, because the rain of bullets went across the forest horizontally—back and forth. The line of fire seemed to be about five feet above the ground, so we stayed low and mostly crawled through the ruts and furrows, staying behind trees as much as possible.

The bullets made a whizzing sound as they passed by, and one zinged past my right ear, so close

I could feel a breeze on my cheek as it barely missed me. Through all this, Mother kept urging us to keep moving forward no matter what, and we did.

After what seemed like a long time—who knows how long because something like this feels much longer than it is in clock time—the shooting stopped. Luckily none of us had been hit.

We kept walking until, during the very early hours of the morning, we could not move any longer. The children were all exhausted and crying, the adults close to fainting. We had to stop, which we finally did, with no idea which side of the border we were on. Too tired to think of anything but rest, we had exceeded our physical limits and fell asleep as soon as we lay down.

In the morning, we would find out whether the thumb of fate was pointing up or down. Meanwhile, nature claimed its due.

The rest of us were still asleep when Mother got up at dawn and cautiously went to scout the area. After taking several steps, she found herself on the edge of a sheer drop of at least ten feet, which was hard to see because of trees growing on its edge. It was not easily noticeable even in daylight.

This gave her cold chills, she said. If we had not stopped when we did, we would have gone over the edge, starting with the baby carriage.

As she ventured further along the edge of the drop, looking for a way down, she suddenly heard voices below. Hiding behind bushes and trees, inching closer to see who was speaking, joy flooded her.

They were speaking English! And as she got even closer, she heard more voices and saw a whole crowd of people milling around. We had made it to the American Zone.

She rushed back to us with the news. All at once no one was tired any more, just eager to find a way down. But wait, we had crossed the border "illegally," and what if they decided to send us back? This had to be done carefully.

The women quietly explored the terrain on both sides, and found a possible descent path far enough away so we wouldn't be entering the camp itself. We would then have to keep silent and out of sight until it was safe to slip in unnoticed. No problem. By now we were all used to stealth. Now that the Soviet threat was over, at least for the time being, I found this adventure rather fun.

After going down the incline, we circled halfway around the camp perimeter and then quietly blended into the movement of people around the camp.

We split into two family groups to avoid drawing undue attention and located a place to leave our things. Having left the baggage wagon behind in the barn, we now had to carry our luggage, and all the children would have to walk.

We joined a long food line winding toward an open service tent with a wood-fed stove and huge cooking pots. The dishes we used were metal army gear. Looking at the number of tents we could see, Mother figured the camp could probably house at least several hundred people. Some kind of porridge was being served for breakfast when we arrived, with an allotment of bread and condensed milk for children. To us, this was a banquet. We had hardly eaten for a long time.

I welcomed the meal but was wary of the Americans, even though the people doling out food seemed nice. They were mostly women, and not in uniform. As my mother had promised, they were helping us, but it was only yesterday that we were dodging bullets fired by their soldiers. I could still hear the sound of their whizzing by.

This was my first interaction with Americans close up, not counting Sarge and the other soldiers, and I was not ready to trust them yet. Even though they were smiling and feeding us now, I felt it best to be cautious. What if they had killed us? What if they changed again tomorrow?

My mind could not wrap itself around all these contradictions. If you had asked me at that moment if I would ever want to live in America, I would have answered with a resounding "No."

Chapter 9

NON-REPATRIABLE

Where we landed turned out to be a triage center populated by refugees of various nationalities, all "Displaced Persons," DPs for short—our new official designation. The camp was temporary, awaiting the American command's plan for what to do with us.

Meanwhile, we were all documented and put on a list of people needing more permanent housing, catalogued according to nationality.

Our food was supplied by UNRRA (United Nations Relief and Rehabilitation Association), an organization that set up the camps to take care of over a million DPs still homeless and stateless after millions of others had returned to their former homes, either voluntarily or under duress. Their fate after they returned was unknown, though word got out that many were killed, imprisoned, or deprived of their property and freedom.

After we ate, we stood in another line to register for permanent camp assignment. Since the final sorting out of who would go where was actually done in Munich, the main triage center for southern Germany, we were given a pass to travel there for permanent placement. But how? Rail travel was not yet fully restored, and we couldn't pay the fare anyway.

Mother asked if there was any other available transportation, given how exhausted the children and the elders were. And if we had to walk and sleep outdoors again, would that be a problem under their rules? The person doing the registering didn't know the answers.

She asked to speak to the camp commander, and was directed to a building at the edge of the camp. The clerk doubted that she could get an audience.

We waited again while she walked to "headquarters," and in less than an hour she came back smiling.

"Thank God I speak some English," she said.

The officer had been very nice and given her an authorization slip to ride on military trucks if they had empty space in the back—if the driver was willing. Mother was sure that would not be a problem. Now that the war was over, American soldiers would surely be glad to help a group of women and children in need. Remembering Sarge, I didn't share her optimism, but kept silent and hoped she was right.

At first, as we stood on the roadside when a truck approached, a few did stop, but most drove by without even looking at us. As they passed, we noticed that many had lots of empty space in back—driver's choice, as Mother had been warned. Disappointed each time, we kept walking until we saw another truck. Same experience. We were authorized to get rides, so why were so few drivers stopping?

We discovered the answer by accident while resting in the shade of a high hedge. Mother stood by the road to try again in case a truck came by.

When she saw one and made the usual signal, the truck stopped immediately and the two soldiers in front eagerly invited her to join them. Their fallen faces when she called to us to come were priceless. *All* of us? They had seen only Mother. To their credit, they accepted this unexpected cargo gracefully, after being shown the authorization slip from the triage camp.

When we arrived at their next destination, they eagerly helped us off the truck. Mother immediately embarked on her usual quest, this time to the officer in charge of this new town's military cohort. She told the story of that meeting with amusement when she returned.

Their meeting had included a mild "culture shock." The American army had taken over the town mayor's office, and a soldier in the crowded waiting area told her in broken German that the "chief" was too busy to see anyone. Furthermore, there was no translator and since none of the supplicants spoke any English, he couldn't talk to them anyway.

Mother responded in emphatic English that in fact she *did* speak English. The soldier looked dubious but with his rationale for refusing negated, led her to the door that shielded the "too busy" chief.

A loud shout responded to her knock: "Do you speak English?"

"Yes," she shouted back as confidently as she could muster.

Her English was elementary at best, the product of several years of school instruction and a brief stay in England, but it would have to do.

"Okay, come in then!"

Facing her as she entered were the bottoms of his army boots on the table, the rest of him almost invisible as he leaned back in a carved office chair. He didn't move, just waved her forward to where he could see her better. As more of him emerged, she noticed that he was busily chewing gum.

We were not familiar with chewing gum in Europe, and she was used to men standing up in the presence of a lady, or at least sitting up if they were elderly or very important, so his attitude and behavior took her aback.

Once they started talking, however, she said he did sit up and was quite helpful. She returned with a housing assignment as well as a new perspective on cultural differences.

Life was simpler after that because the American authorities made space somewhere in every town for DPs with proper ID, often angering local residents who were ordered to take us in when asked. Being forced on people was awkward, but we didn't have other options, so we tried to be as quiet and non-intrusive as possible. That usually helped smooth things, especially with several German speakers in our group. And, as always, some locals were kinder and more accepting than others.

A quirky image from one of these stopover towns stayed with me. We had just arrived. While our "caravan" settled around a bench along the main street to wait, Mother went off to find the officer in charge of DPs.

She headed left, and I watched her walk quite a distance before blending into the street crowd. We waited a long time—or so it seemed to me, nervous whenever Mother was out of sight. I kept looking for her to come back.

Suddenly, Mamma grabbed my arm and pointed: "Look, there's your mother!"

She was pointing to a tank rolling down the street from our left, heading right. Standing in the opening on top was Mother, with a soldier next to her.

She was only visible above the waist, and my first response was fear—was she being taken away? But then I noticed that she was talking with him in what seemed a friendly way. As they passed, she turned and waved, smiling at us, so I knew it was okay. Now I was free to be impressed by her riding in a *tank*.

As always, her lodging search was successful, but the first thing we did when she returned was to ply her with questions.

"How did you get on the tank? Were you scared? Where did you go? Why did it take so long?"

"Slow down, one at a time. There was a long line at the command center, and the tank ride saved me from a very long walk to the other end of town. The soldiers were nice enough to drive me, and all they had was a tank." Her tone was matter-of-fact.

"But how come they offered you a ride? You're not a soldier."

"It was nothing special. I ran into a couple of soldiers after leaving you and asked for directions. They told me the headquarters was way at the other end of town. I must have looked tired because then one of them said they were about to take the tank back there and I was welcome to ride with them. They teased me about being too scared to ride in a tank, so of course I had to say yes. It's uncomfortable to get up to the top where you saw me, but they helped. They were all very nice. I walked back. That's the whole story."

One of the grandmothers chimed in with a chuckle, "And of course they would have made me the same offer if I had asked for directions? Or a man in your situation?"

Mother's appearance probably did elicit the offer, but I had noticed that without trying, by just being herself, she seemed to be easily liked by both sexes, so that wasn't the whole reason. I thought it was more about her being a nice person.

In any case, this town stayed in my mind because of the tank ride, and it turned out to be our last stop on the way to Munich, where we would get our permanent camp assignment. Thanks to the increasing military traffic on the main roads, we covered this final stretch quickly.

What stood out for me during this final travel segment was my first Hershey bar. It had been a long time since my last taste of chocolate.

During a short stop for a break, I became fascinated as I watched a black soldier near the truck washing his hands. Having never seen anyone of another race before, it puzzled me why his hands were not getting "clean." And his whole skin was dark brown.

So I asked my mother, who laughed and explained that some of the Americans had originally come from a place called Africa, where everyone had brown skin. To my perpetual "why," she responded that it got really hot there and the sun wouldn't burn darker skin as easily as white. That made sense.

The man saw me watching him and smiled. He had very white teeth and a very nice smile. When he finished his task, he reached into a sack next to him, pulled out a Hershey bar and offered it to me. I wasn't sure at first what it was, so I looked inquiringly at Mother.

She nodded and smiled at the soldier, saying "Thank you for the chocolate."

Chocolate! I had the impulse to grab and unwrap this unexpected gift immediately, but remembered my manners and took the offered gift with a curtsy. He seemed a bit surprised, then smiled again.

A whole bar just for me! I would probably have to share it, but it was still a very good day.

This man was the nicest American I had met so far. I supposed that some of them were probably nice and some not, just like the Germans I'd met—and for that matter, the Estonians I'd known. The world was such a puzzle. You could never tell right away who was nice and who wasn't.

But life was getting better. I had a chocolate bar to prove it.

Chapter 10

SETTLING IN LIMBO

We spent two weeks at our second triage camp in
Munich while waiting for a "permanent" assignment. I became entranced with the city, especially
the famous clock in the big square with its musical
chimes and moving figures.

Since we were not confined to the camp and had
an easy tram connection to the city center, my culture
maven mother lost no time in taking in as much as
we could of this classically Bavarian city.

And it was just she and I alone on these excursions, while Mamma watched the baby. What joy! It
had been such a long, scary time since I'd had Mother all to myself, and now we tried to do something
for a few hours every day between Baby's feedings.
Summer weather made it even more enjoyable. I was
sorry when we received our camp assignment and
had to leave.

We had hoped to find some information about Father at one of these camps, but he was not on any lists.
We hardly ever talked about him because there was

nothing to say except that we missed him, and it was too painful to say out loud that he might be dead.

So we focused on the task at hand. It almost seemed as though keeping hope alive required that we hold the thought of his death at bay.

This time we were provided with transportation in a convoy of army trucks carrying DP's to their designated camps. It was close to my seventh birthday when we arrived in Augsburg and settled into our quarters.

It had been almost a year since we left Tallinn, but it felt like forever. Our traveling companions were no longer with us. I was happy to be with just my own family, and it also meant an end to my having to look after the smaller children. Being praised for being mature beyond my years had been nice, but it still felt like a lot of responsibility.

Our first housing assignment in Augsburg was a fairly large room, one of a row of rooms in a long building facing the top of a hill across the street, with a large field covered with high grass beyond. A path worn through the grass by long-term use cut diagonally across to the far end, where local Germans lived. It was often used as a shortcut to walk from camp to the city. The street in front of our building formed one border of the camp.

We had a small wood stove in our room where Mamma prepared food. Bathroom arrangements were communal. The building itself was part of a square block of housing that had been inhabited by German workers and recently cleared by the occupation authorities to create the camp.

There were a number of such housing blocks, with an inner courtyard for storing firewood and drying laundry on designated lines for each building. It also provided safe play space for children.

By this time, we had barely any worldly goods left, and the CARE packages from abroad that started arriving on a weekly basis, along with shipments of donated clothing, were a godsend. I finally got a new pair of shoes. As the days went by, we began to adjust to the rhythm of this new life, met new people, and settled into a daily routine.

Since this particular camp, in a suburb called Hochfeld, was only for refugees from the three Baltic countries of Estonia, Latvia, and Lithuania, each with its own section of housing blocks, we found ourselves once more among Estonians.

I was thrilled to hear my native language around me. Finally I could again communicate freely with people other than my family. And there were lots of children of various ages to play with and get to know. One day followed another, with a lot to do and absorb, not the least of which was working with the other residents of our building to create communal guidelines for using hot water, bath facilities, and cleaning bathrooms.

As children, we were not directly involved in this. We were busy checking each other out, forming new friendships, and creating games to play. All this was a huge relief from the tension and exhaustion of the months we had just lived through.

As the weeks passed, we slowly settled into a new "normalcy," each attending to her daily tasks.

Mamma, Queen of the "kitchen" corner of the room, magically manifested surprisingly good meals from whatever emerged from our CARE packages. Spam became a frequent base for her alchemy, but to my delight there was also one Hershey bar in every package.

Mother tended the baby and made our living space as attractive and welcoming as possible, given one room with three mattresses plus baby carriage covering much of the floor surface.

I mostly played outside in the balmy late-summer warmth with newfound friends, except when curled up with a book. Any kind of book I could borrow would do, not necessarily one meant for children. Since many of our fellow DPs had also brought along a couple of favorite books, trading back and forth expanded everyone's reading horizons.

There were always flowers in our living space, picked from empty lots or nearby woods, as there had been throughout our escape odyssey. The war had broken down much of civilization's infrastructure and the re-emerging bare earth lost no time in sprouting new growth—mostly weeds, but many of them in spring bloom. Whenever we spent more than a single night indoors, Mother had managed to scavenge an empty can or thrown-away jar and fill it with a few blooms and greenery to decorate our space.

One time during our long walk, as we were settling for the night in yet another temporary shelter, Mother and I had been about to leave on our flower quest when Mamma asked, "You're exhausted. Why do you bother?"

Mother turned briefly. "To remember who I am," she replied.

And yet there was a pall on all our activities, cast by the "elephant in the room." The unspoken question of Father's fate weighed heavily on our hearts. Where was he? I sometimes thought I heard Mother crying at night. Sometimes I cried, too.

Yet in the daytime, we all smiled and braved on while time passed and hope faded.

The most memorable day of our first months in camp began peacefully. I was curled up on my mattress, reading. Baby slept in her carriage. Mother dusted near the window.

Suddenly, she let out a loud *"Issand Jumal!"* (Oh my God!), dropped her dust cloth on the floor, and rushed out the door like a sprinting doe spooked by a wolf.

Shocked upright, I ran to the door she had left wide open. I saw her running full tilt down the path across the field heading toward town. My mother never ran like that—or raised her voice. This was so out of character that it frightened me.

I then noticed near the other end of the path the figures of two men walking toward the camp. When one of them saw Mother, he dropped his suitcase and they both raced toward each other until they collided. Or so it seemed.

It wasn't until he was spinning her around in his arms that I recognized who it was. Father had found us! He was alive!

I didn't know what to make of their strange behavior, though, since I had never seen them act like that. "Nordic reserve" had usually prevailed in our home. And I had surprisingly mixed feelings about seeing Father again, now that we were out of danger.

Even though I had prayed for his safety and hoped he would find us, I couldn't forget that he had not been there when we desperately needed him. That such a powerful man could not have chosen to do something he really wanted to do was something my mind still could not take in, regardless of Mother's explanations.

He looked so happy to see me when he came in the door, but I suddenly felt shy. Instead of running into his arms, I approached haltingly and politely held out my hand. Disappointment flashed across his face, but only for a moment. Then he crouched down to my level and solemnly took my hand.

"I am so happy to see you. You have grown—and your mother told me how brave you were through such a difficult time when she needed your help."

He looked at me tenderly, and added with emphasis: "I am *very* proud of you."

His approval pleased me, but I also felt like crying. Confused and embarrassed, I retreated to my book and hid my face behind it.

He didn't follow or try to "make it better," letting me adjust to his arrival in my own way. Just turned seven, I was dealing with complex emotions I had no words for.

Had I been back in my childhood home, I would have immediately gone to my inner friend Ome behind Mother's mirror and hung out with her until I sorted things out, but that was not an option now. It never occurred to me that in a different way I could have created a similar make-believe refuge for myself where I was.

With Father's arrival, our lives changed. With a fifth person in a room designated for a maximum of four, another mattress on the floor made walking around even more awkward. In addition, a man living with us at such close quarters made modesty something we suddenly had to think about. It had not been an issue with an all-female traveling group.

Of course, there was no privacy for my parents either to be with each other alone, but I liked eavesdropping on their conversations. To me, the privacy issue only meant dressing and undressing more carefully when Father was in the room, and that was not a problem.

To my surprise, Mamma suddenly became keen on short excursions into Augsburg, usually during the early afternoon when the baby was sleeping after a nursing session.

She invited me along to explore the city, its shops and "beautiful buildings," most of which turned out to be churches, not at the head of my list. As a devoted Lutheran, in a city associated with Martin Luther, it was a thrill for her, I guessed. For me it was something new so I went along, still puzzled why a homebody like her suddenly became such an avid explorer.

Mother and Father liked to take walks alone, too, which made me feel left out, and I figured that's what they'd be doing while we were gone. Our family walks on Sundays were highlights of the week.

It helped that Father often took time with me to discuss the books I was reading or whatever else spurred my interest, but he never talked about where he had been or how he reached us. Whenever I tried to ask, he quickly turned the conversation back to me.

Slowly, I began to feel more at ease again with him, now that he was back in our lives and promised to stay. He had felt almost like a stranger when he first arrived.

Chapter 11

NORMALCY BUBBLE

All the camps managed by UNRRA were temporary stopgap accommodations for Displaced Persons like us who were stranded until we could find somewhere else in the world to emigrate.

We were called non-repatriable because we would face imprisonment or death at the hands of the Soviets if we returned to our occupied homelands. Around six million others whose countries had been liberated, or who themselves were liberated from concentration camps, prisons, or forced army enlistments, had already returned home, many to a questionable fate.

There was a collaborative effort between the Allied Command, UNRRA, and the DPs themselves to create a semblance of normal community within the camps, especially for the benefit of children. Their highest priority was to create camp schools or to enroll us in the local German school. Since the numbers of school-age children and adolescents in many of the camps would have overwhelmed the local schools, they decided to create separate in-camp schools for each nationality.

In our camp, Father became involved in two things that happened quickly.

First, a system of internal self-government was established, led by a governing committee for each nationality: Estonian, Latvian, and Lithuanian. They were to organize social structures and solve problems within the camp, in collaboration with the official administration. Second, both a primary and a secondary school were established in each of the camp sections, with instruction in our own native languages and English as a required course.

Father was appointed or elected to the governing committee for the Estonian section, and also became a founder of the secondary school. All children were required to enroll, to make sure we would have the necessary schooling to transfer into the educational stream wherever we emigrated.

There was no lack of qualified teachers for these schools. The camp was full of displaced professionals with no outlet for their skills. They welcomed the opportunity. The array of intellectuals, artists, scientists, teachers, musicians, and skilled craftsmen concentrated within those few crowded blocks was remarkable. We were what Stalin called the "refuse" he would have killed outright or worked to death in Siberia.

Father's role in these activities brought a welcome improvement in our housing. We were reassigned from our cramped quarters into an apartment in a block of three-story apartment buildings from which the local German workers had been evicted.

For us, this new housing was a real boon. Each apartment had two bedrooms, a spacious eat-in kitchen that became our common living area, and a bathroom.

Our family of four got the larger room, while Mamma shared the smaller one with a nice handicapped woman and her teen-aged son. That made seven of us sharing this small apartment, but it felt luxurious. There was even some storage space in the basement for our suitcases.

We had beds, a wood stove with an oven, and a wood-fired water heater with an allotment of logs sufficient for everyone to have a weekly hot bath. Not a home as we had known it in Estonia, but a wonderful contrast to the year we had just lived through.

Since the evicted occupants had been forced to leave most of the furnishings behind, taking only personal belongings, all the basic necessities were there for our use.

As time drifted toward autumn, the weather cooled and the newly created schools opened. Their structure and curriculum were based, as much as possible, on the pre-Soviet Estonian school system.

I was two years younger than the others in my class, but this placement worked well over the next four years, both academically and socially. It kept me interested in class, and I felt comfortable with my classmates. I didn't really feel the age difference.

The secondary school, *gümnaasium* in Estonian, opened shortly thereafter, in an attic room where the classes had to meet on different schedules because of limited space, and students held cups to catch the rainfall dripping through the roof during wet weather. But the teacher line-up was impressive, with not only well-qualified secondary teachers but also university faculty teaching their subject specialties. Fortunately for the teachers, they were paid a small but much appreciated stipend.

Father taught mathematics and physics at the secondary school. In addition to teaching their subject, each teacher was a "class elder" who personally mentored a particular group of students from entry through graduation. This fostered consistent and often enduring bonds.

The classes had a mixed age range, depending on when each student's schooling had been interrupted, and how long they had been wandering as refugees.

With all the camp schools' limitations—scant supplies, improvised texts, and lack of library resources—a teacher's ability to directly share his or her own knowledge and life experience was the key to students' progress.

That was no easy task in that makeshift situation, with war-scarred teenagers trying to get back into a normal life after their traumatic survival struggles. Yet somehow it worked.

For me, camp life took on a comforting daily rhythm: a predictable cycle of school, after-school play outdoors in good weather, family dinner and conversation, homework, evening reading, and bedtime. Sundays were either leisurely or filled with family activities, and occasional events like a theater or musical performance, visiting friends, or an excursion to town and the surrounding countryside.

As I had at the wartime work camp, I found ways to have fun and a group of friends to play with. But this was so much better than being fenced in and afraid all the time. I was on the way to becoming a child again. I had tried so hard to be grown up during our flight to freedom.

Christmas was the best. We always managed to have a tree with homemade ornaments and real candles carefully held in place by special clips.

My happiest Christmas was when Mother somehow managed to find a lovely doll to replace the one I had brought from Estonia but lost so soon after our arrival in Germany. She had a pretty porcelain face and was exactly the right size for me to hold. I played with her often—rather, she played with friends' dolls, as we lent and borrowed doll clothes to vary their wardrobes.

Gifts in general were handmade necessities— sweaters, socks, mittens—but, for me, the most special gift every Christmas was a new doll outfit that Mother had secretly sown or knit.

Mamma always baked delicious cookies and the traditional Christmas *kringel*, a braided sweetbread with raisins and nuts, from ingredients saved in bits and pieces throughout the previous months.

I also loved the Christmas concerts and group singing, often with children performing carols and folk dances. It was a time we excitedly waited for all year.

All kinds of groups formed in the camp: a men's chorus, a women's chorus, a small orchestra, a theatre group, folk-dancing groups for adults and children, sports (volleyball and basketball in particular),

craft circles, music lessons, art instruction, and whatever else someone thought up. These activities were
uncompensated except for those suitable for barter,
like "I'll give your child piano lessons if you'll tutor
mine in math."

Cooperation was the name of the game, and resources were often pooled for mutual benefit. I heard
my parents say that a likely basis for this remarkable
level of cooperation and harmony in our difficult circumstances was that we were all in the same boat.
We all had little beyond the bare necessities, so we
held each other afloat as best we could.

There were certainly some feuds and disagree-
ments, especially about "the best way" to do things—
an old adage says that for three Estonians to make
a decision requires two committees. Nevertheless,
the relative absence of wide "have" and "have not"
disparities cut down on competitiveness and made
room for our better natures to run the show most of
the time.

With Father teaching full-time and serving on the
governing committee, it seemed he was always going
out after dinner to some kind of meeting. If it wasn't
about school or camp, it was about his active role in
church. Several congregations had formed, with cler-
gy at the camp conducting services.

Mother also joined all kinds of activities, like choral singing, leather-craft, and refashioning donated
clothing into something that fit well and looked presentable. Most women at the camp participated in
this fashion remodeling so skillfully that one would

never have pegged us, at casual glance, as destitute refugees.

Mother also served as leader of the camp's YWCA branch and was sponsored one year to attend a multinational conference. Never a joiner of groups in Estonia, this was new to her, but she seemed to enjoy it. Maybe it was a way of forgetting her worries for a while.

The adults lovingly created and maintained a virtual "normalcy bubble" for us children. In effect, we lived in a temporary "virtual Estonia" surrounded by ominous happenings, which I sensed but was never told about.

The older children knew more and were not as careful about not talking when younger ones were around, so we got intimations of NKVD (KGB) activities around us, but when some people occasionally disappeared and we asked where they had gone, the adults gave vague answers and changed the subject.

Only once, after I repeatedly asked about the sudden death of a wonderful violinist friend of theirs, did my parents actually tell me that he chose to die by his own hand rather than be "repatriated." No one knew why he was chosen. The whole process seemed arbitrary.

I was shocked and cried, but at least I now understood my parents' visible distress. The idea of suicide had never touched my life before.

Chapter 12

CAMPING IN QUARANTINE

Mostly, these years in limbo were relatively carefree for children like me who lived with their own families, or at least with one parent.

Those who had lost both parents in the war had been sent away to special camps for orphans so we never met them. The few who lived in our camp had been "adopted" by friends or relatives and were probably passed off officially as their own.

We all lived close to each other, so there was never a shortage of playmates. We had our squabbles and best friends, but most of our out-of-school energy went into a variety of sports and games.

There was a spirit of camaraderie even with the Latvian and Lithuanian children, with whom we had a language barrier but whose equal right to play in our common "no-man's-land" areas on the fringes of the camp we respected. Not all of our activities would have found favor with our parents, however—had they known.

Early on, some of us had explored the uninhabited area beyond the Estonian section by following a high wire fence across the street from our apartment building past the Latvians and Lithuanians as far as it went. Railroad tracks ran parallel to the fence on its other side, with a few railroad cars still strewn about. It had been a transportation center before it was bombed.

When we reached the end of the camp, there was another stretch of more intact railroad track that provided an irresistible invitation to test our balancing skills. Walking these tracks led to our first big discovery, ruins of the Messerschmitt airplane factory. The wrecked buildings were fun to explore and the remaining pieces of wall to climb.

The best part was finding potential playthings in the debris of airplane parts scattered throughout the grounds. Our favorite discovery was a semi-intact engine that still had a full propeller attached.

A group of us managed to get it upright with the propeller horizontally on top, the engine supported by rocks and other debris we piled around it for stability. We added makeshift steps made of small boulders to climb on the propeller. This opus functioned as a sort of carousel, with one or two of us sitting on the blades and others spinning us around.

Since we had to take turns spinning and being spun, this activity occupied us for hours at a time. The line of eager participants was often long.

A group of boys, continually into war games, constructed "bunkers" and other accoutrements of warfare. With children of all three camp sections using their creativity in turn, over time all kinds of weird and wonderful structures emerged from the ruins.

What we didn't know, until one unlucky boy found out the hard way and lost a finger, was that there were also live hand grenades and other ammunition among the rubbish. He accidentally set one off, not knowing what it was. I didn't know him and heard about it later.

It must have been what alerted parents throughout the camp to the dangers of our secret playground, and the announcment at school that the Messerschmitt field was now off limits to all of us—an order that was sobering but didn't entirely stop the games there. It did thin the crowd, though.

Our main focus now shifted to the woods nearby, especially to a large bomb crater with a fallen tree about a foot in diameter directly across its middle. To us, the crater's depth of about seven feet made walking across risky enough to be exciting. It promised a nasty fall if we failed, so there were more watchers than walkers.

I was one of the latter, and crossed many times. Although I seemed foolhardy to some friends, it was actually a carefully calculated risk. Having climbed anything available since infancy, I knew in my gut when it was okay and when to stop. After a while, it was no longer exciting.

As extracurricular activities became available, my parents signed me up for piano lessons, taught by our school music teacher on a donated vintage upright in the music classroom. She had about a dozen students, and we were each scheduled for half-hour practice sessions several times a week after school.

I was not an enthusiastic piano student, but my

parents felt it would be good for me, so I half-heartedly attended practice.

When the weather was nice, however, I would
sometimes arrive for the session and, after the previous student was safely gone, climb out through the
ground-floor window, returning in time to be found
practicing when the next student arrived. Somehow
I managed to make enough progress to stay within a
sufficient range of acceptable mediocrity, and never
got caught.

Realizing that this opportunity was an effort for
my parents made me feel guilty, but the lure of the
outdoors in good weather was irresistible.

I preferred the Girl Scouts, as well as folk dancing
and sports like dodge ball and volleyball, so I became
a *hellake* (Brownie) to participate in these activities.
Our small troop was affiliated with the international scouting organization, as scouting in free Estonia
had been, and during the summer I turned eight they
arranged for us to go camping.

That was to be the first time I went anywhere
outside the camp without a parent, but the thought
of the fun we would have won out over separation
anxiety. The decision to go was my own.

We set up camp in a beautiful forest clearing part-
way up a mountainside in the Alpine foothills. There
was a shallow brook to wade in, a bracing experience
for feet not used to ice-cold water straight from the
mountain snow, and therefore an opportunity for "I
dare you" games that most of us avoided.

We had enough balls to play with so we didn't
have to endlessly wait our turn—sheer heaven—and

better food than ever before since leaving Estonia.
Dessert every day! Sleeping in borrowed army tents
was exciting. Younger ones like me slept on cots in
big tents, with seven per tent plus an adult, and older
ones paired up in little pup tents.

I was surprised to find camp so much fun that I
hardly missed my family. That was a milestone shift.
In spite of the trauma of our escape journey, my sense
of security had now grown enough to allow for separation from family without panic over losing them.

The timing of this shift in me could not have been
better, because this first separation, supposed to last
a week, turned out to be much longer.

Two days before we were to go home, one of the
older girls got very sick and was taken to a hospital.
We were never told what was wrong with her, but
the Red Cross was concerned about the possibility
of an epidemic spreading through the camps, especially since the supply of medicine in general, and
antibiotics like penicillin in particular, was totally in-
adequate.

Everything, including food and medicine, was in
short supply or non-existent in Europe during those
postwar years, and the spread of any contagious disease could be a disaster. The decision was made to
quarantine the whole camp, with no one coming in
or out.

We were able to continue our games and activities
until it was time to leave, though, with our leaders
watching us closely for any sign of impending illness.

Fortunately, no such signs emerged, but we were
told that we couldn't go home until they were sure

none of us were carrying the disease. There were no drugs or other preventive measures available so we would have to be quarantined in a hospital for two weeks. If no one showed any symptoms by the end of that time, we would be safe to go back to our families.

A wave of fear swept over the camp. What was a quarantine? And why couldn't we see our parents? Would we be locked up? Taken far away? Put in a prison camp?

We imagined dire scenarios, despite assurances by our leaders that we would all stay together and be fine. We couldn't have direct contact with our parents, true, but they could come to visit, and we could see each other at a distance.

We agreed that it still sounded suspicious, but okay—we would wait and see. I decided to not think about my fear and enjoy the rest of camp time as much as possible. Most of us rallied, and the ball games and evening songfests around the campfire went on until our departure.

As we were packing to leave, some of the girls got upset and cried while the rest of us tried to cheer them up—whether they were sad about the quarantine or having to leave camp, I wasn't sure.

Army trucks drove us to a hospital on the outskirts of Augsburg, where hospital staff, wearing masks and rubber gloves, walked us straight to the top floor, which had been cleared, cleaned, and disinfected in preparation for our arrival. No one was allowed to go near anyone who was not with our camp group.

Only medical personnel needed for monitoring us and bringing food or supplies would enter and leave our floor during those two weeks. Parents could come at a designated time each day and wave to us from the lawn below our windows. They could also write to us and send books or toys, but once inside the hospital, the items couldn't be returned. Nothing we touched could go out, including letters.

When our parents visited, as most of them faithfully did, we tried to talk back and forth, but the distance made it difficult, and there were too many of us talking at the same time. We settled for smiles, waves, and blown kisses.

Even with all the restrictions, these visits were the highlight of my day, and my parents always came. It was not easy for them. They had to take several trams, and that cost money as well as time waiting for connections. Father had to rush directly from school to make it within the visiting hour. This was a German hospital, so time limits were strictly enforced.

For me, the dependability of seeing them every day made all the difference. It made me feel safe and I started to enjoy the freedom to play with new board games and drawing supplies donated by an unknown organization.

To compensate for the lack of fresh air and outdoor exercise, we learned folk dances and songs to perform for our parents when our quarantine was lifted. Meanwhile, our leaders found many ingenious ways to channel our youthful energies.

I also decided to use Mother's absence to experiment with something I couldn't do at home. Mrs. M, the mother of one of my friends whose hair was always curly like I wanted mine to be, was the head of our troupe and therefore quarantined with us. I saw her wind and tie her daughter's hair around rag strips while she slept, which produced curls when she removed them in the morning. I knew that was what a lot of grownup women did. I had asked Mother if she could do it for me, but she said I was too young.

Now was my chance. I asked Mrs. M if she could curl my hair, to see how it looked. To my delight, she agreed. Of course, she didn't know that my mother had refused. So we did it one night, and the next morning, I did indeed have curls.

I thought I looked pretty glamorous, and tossed my head the way the older girls did, to make my hair bounce when I walked. When visiting time came, I hoped Mother wouldn't notice my new hairdo from that distance, but she spotted it immediately.

"Did you curl your hair?"

She shouted loud enough for me to hear, but I pretended I couldn't and just smiled at her.

She wagged her finger at me, but I could tell she was not really angry. She shook her head and sort of smiled.

When they left, I skipped down the hallway to my room, tossing my curls left and right, savoring what felt like a victory. The curlers were uncomfortable to sleep with, though, so I didn't ask Mrs. M to do it again. My curiosity had been satisfied and I decided it was fine to wait till I was older. Maybe someone would invent better curlers by then.

The leaders never showed their worry that someone would get sick and they would have to keep us confined longer. Their ingenuity in keeping us interested and busy while stuck indoors was amazing.

Thankfully, we all stayed healthy, and our unexpected camping extension turned out to be an adventure. As objects of sympathy to the volunteers serving with help agencies, we received several packages of goodies and toys during our confinement, so in fact we were more spoiled than victimized.

Wait till our friends heard about *this*. We all had lots of stories to tell.

Yet we all cheered when our two weeks were up. The doors were finally unlocked and we could leave. Freedom was sweet. Our parents waited outside with hugs and kisses. It was time to go back "home" and resume our normal school routine, garnished with all the other activities the camp had to offer, or conjured up by us.

To complete the happy ending, we found out some weeks later that the girl whose illness had prompted the quarantine recovered fully.

Chapter 13

Ill Winds

The DPs' lack of employment and loss of identity sparked a percolating pot of artistic expression, using whatever means and materials were available.

My most magical memories were of being taken to the theater at night to see an operetta or play. *The Merry Widow* was my favorite. To my chagrin, most dramatic plays were off limits because I was "too young." I saw myself as quite grown up, so I protested, but to no avail.

Some local Germans attended the operettas and expressed amazement at the quality of sets, costumes, and performances. Their reaction was warranted. Costumes had to be hand sewn and patched together from clothing scrounged from IRO donation boxes. The sets were a *tour de force* of creating convincing illusions from scrap.

The level of performance was less surprising, since we had in our camp the second most famous soprano in Estonia, a well-known tenor, and an up-and-coming baritone. Nor was there a lack of other good singing voices for backup. Choral singing had been a national passion in Estonia for many generations, so a well-trained voice was not hard to find. The camp choral groups often toured other camps to give concerts.

I became one of four girls who participated in various cultural events dressed in folk costumes. My mother had constructed my costume by hand from various scraps of material, starting with a cut-up wool blanket, but the finished product looked good, especially from a distance. Its finishing touch was a picturesque embroidered headdress. Our task was to curtsy and present performers and conductors with a bouquet of flowers at the end of every performance.

I became quite adept at this, and the practice of being in front of an audience helped me manage stage fright at other gatherings where we had to dance or recite poetry. The hard work and ingenuity that went into creating my folk costume was rewarded by the poise I gained while wearing it for these events.

This relatively pleasant period was suddenly interrupted when, with no warning, pestilence raged through the camp and a series of contagious childhood illnesses swept through the schools. Medicine was unavailable to us, so I went through whooping cough, chicken pox, and then measles.

I recovered from the first two, but the measles hung on and led to serious complications.

I was now eight years old. My whole body morphed into a coarse surface of red bumpy rash, as I sweated in bed with a high fever for what felt like endless days and nights. An Estonian doctor in the camp did what he could, but all he had to offer was palliative care and aspirin.

I developed a middle ear infection on both sides, and when it didn't pass and my right ear got worse and more painful, he went to the camp authorities and insisted that I be taken to a hospital with surgical capacity. The infection had spread past the inner ear, raising the potential for brain infection. If it progressed far enough, it could prove fatal.

It took several days, but finally an ambulance arrived and took me, with Mother at my side, to a German hospital. I was terrified, but Mother stayed with me through the x-rays and blood tests.

My ear infection was serious, but could have been cured with penicillin, except there wasn't any available—at least not for us. The U.S. Army had a supply, but only for its own people. The German doctors had no option but surgery.

The x-ray uncovered a bigger problem. The infection had infiltrated not just the inner ear canal but much deeper, into the mastoid bone behind the ear. They would have to drill into the bone, clean out the infection, and hope to avoid damage to the brain itself.

The surgery would be complicated and risky, with a chance of permanent damage to brain tissue, depending on how deep the infection had penetrated. The doctor couldn't guarantee they would get it all.

On the other hand, without the surgery I might not live. In view of this, they wanted to go ahead immediately. With trepidation, Mother gave her consent. The urgency didn't even give her time to go home and consult Father, and there were no telephones at the camp.

I was beyond scared, even without being aware at first of how grave my condition really was. All I knew about surgery was that they would cut me with a knife, and that was terrifying.

Thank goodness my little sister was now big enough to be with Mamma, so Mother could stay with me at the hospital. I couldn't imagine going through this without her. I couldn't even talk with the doctors. Whatever German I had learned earlier was now mostly gone. I had to be brave again. Could I?

I was told that the surgery would remove the infection that was making me sick, and after staying in the hospital for a while I would be well again. Then they wheeled me into the operating room and started to prepare me for administering ether.

Panicked, I refused to let go of Mother's hand, so the surgeon yielded to her plea to stay with me while I was "going to sleep." I clutched her hand like a lifeline as she spoke to me gently, telling me it wouldn't hurt. Everything would be all right after it was over and I had healed.

Her presence calmed me enough to allow the staff to position me for the surgery. I balked when they put on the mask, and Mother talked me through that, too.

"The mask has some funny-smelling stuff for you to breathe in," she said soothingly in Estonian. "If you don't fight it, you will go to sleep quickly and not feel any pain. Maybe you'll even have a nice dream."

Then, prompted by the surgeon, she told me to count out loud with each breath, and so I did: *"Üks, kaks, kolm, neli, viis, kuus, seitse ...."*

I have no idea how high I counted before succumbing. Going under with ether was like sinking into a deep, dark, spinning hole. The staff got fuzzier and more distant as I dropped down. The voices sounded like echoes far, far away. My vision went black but I could still hear the voices and strange noises, farther and farther away, until they turned into a fading hum.

Finally all sound died and I floated into a darkly luminous nowhere. At the bottom of the spinning funnel, there was no longer any movement, just a deep, peaceful stillness that was not unpleasant— and the next thing I knew, I woke up.

The moment I was aware I was back, I looked for Mother. I couldn't move my head, which was wrapped in thick bandages, but I didn't need to. Her smiling face was right there in front of me, and she was holding my hand.

What a gift it was for me that the surgeon allowed my mother to be right there with me not only when I went under, but again when I woke up. Usually children were picked up and carried off by nursing staff, crying and terrified, into the treatment area, while parents were told to stay in the waiting room. Yet he had been so kind, even though to him we were foreigners.

For the next two weeks I was stuck in a lumpy hospital bed. There was nothing to look at except ugly walls, once probably white, now a dull gray with scuffs and peeled-off paint. I was in a large rectangular room, with a wide hallway opening from its long side toward a nursing station about thirty feet away.

The room was reserved for temporary emergency or post-op recovery patients, so I was usually the only one there, especially at night.

With just a faint glow coming from the hallway, the nights were dark, desolate, and very, very long. I couldn't see what was going on in the hallway, and the only sound was the occasional distant hum of voices.

What I could see included the long blank wall across from my bed, and two mid-sized windows in the shorter walls on each side. Though in need of cleaning, these windows did let in some light but I couldn't turn my head enough to look out. It was deliberately wrapped to be unmovable, angled downward toward the left shoulder, away from the surgical site.

However awkward that made my position, they said it was necessary in order to keep the wound immobile. This not only prevented me from looking out the window, but also made trying to read a book or eat my meals frustrating. Bathroom needs were met with bedpans, and so I didn't get to walk, either—at least for the first week. I felt like a trapped mummy.

I lived for the visiting hour each afternoon when Mother or Father, or both and sometimes Mamma, came to see me.

They read to me, told stories about friends and school, brought books to read together, and in general brightened up the depressing atmosphere I was supposed to heal in. It turned out that I did heal well, probably driven by my burning desire to get out of there.

After two weeks they moved me to a small double room with a door. A young boy from a farm some distance from Augsburg—Mother guessed he was thirteen or so—occupied the other bed. His eyes were both bandaged, also mummy style. They sure liked bandages at that hospital. He was obviously recovering from eye surgery and bored out of his mind by the inability to see or move around.

This set-up was a great improvement. The walls were a yellowish cream color, and the window was cleaner, so for part of the day the sun's rays could penetrate and dance across my wall. That cheered me up.

The boy amused himself by singing songs—endlessly—in a dialect that sounded different from any German I knew. He started in the morning and, with interspersed naps, continued through the day until the staff announced bedtime—the same songs, over and over, stopping only when he heard my parents visiting.

His own parents only came once. I felt sorry for him, and figured they probably lived far away.

Because the "entertainment" in my room was relentless, I slowly, without intending to, started to pick up more and more of the words, and toward the end of my stay I was singing along. I acquired a repertoire of at least half a dozen German songs, with no idea what the words meant.

My pronunciation was apparently quite good, though, according to one young nurse who actually paid attention to us. She seemed to like children more than the others and sometimes stayed beyond her allotted visiting time. When we sang for her, she laughed and asked me if I understood the words.

I said no, and she said it was fine for me to just enjoy the singing. I liked her because she smiled, unlike the dour faces of most of the others—except my doctor, who was always friendly and encouraging. I liked him best.

When it was time to go home, I was so eager I didn't sleep a wink the last night I was there. My roommate had left several days before, and the room became too quiet and lonely. I realized I had enjoyed his company, even though we hadn't been able to talk, just sing.

I decided to give a private concert for my family when I got home to share what I had learned. Mamma and Mother could translate the words and I would finally learn what I had been singing about for so long.

When the time came, my concert did not go as planned. From the first song, I noticed strange reactions from my audience.

Father seemed to have a hard time keeping a straight face, Mamma was frowning, and Mother's face was contorted as though either laughing or crying. I couldn't tell which. Though puzzled and distracted, I carried on with my repertoire.

When I had finished, Mother asked: "Where on earth did you learn those songs?"

I explained about my daily sing-alongs with the boy in the hospital room, which prompted a round of laughter from all three.

"You didn't like my singing?" I felt tears well up. Instead of pleasing them, it seemed I had done something wrong. And now they were laughing at me.

"No, dear, your singing was fine. But do you understand the words of these songs?" Mother's eyes were reassuring. I shook my head.

Father smiled. "Well, the words are not what we would want you to use in front of someone who spoke German. They are not even suitable for adults. The tunes are nice, though, so you can just hum them."

My face must have betrayed disappointment, for he tried to comfort me further: "You learned to pronounce a German dialect that few people can, so you learned a lot. That's good. It will help you in the future to learn other languages more easily."

"Well, it kept you busy when you had nothing to do. I liked your singing." Mamma was no longer frowning, having determined that no moral damage had been done to my youthful innocence. I realized that the words must have been pretty bad. Their strange reactions had been only to the words, not to my performance.

That felt better, but I never sang those songs again.

I had missed a lot of school, and it was time to return. The mummy bandages had come off before I left the hospital, replaced with thinner ones that allowed for movement.

The trouble was that I couldn't turn my neck. It had frozen into an awkward left-facing angle, and I felt embarrassed in front of schoolmates. Over and over they asked,

"What happened to you? Why is your head like that?"

If I told them about the operation, they wanted me to describe all the gory details. I did, a couple of times, but then said no more. I just wanted to forget the whole thing and resume my pre-measles life.

It took another six weeks, and help from a woman in camp who had been trained in physical rehabilitation, before my neck regained some range of motion.

It took much longer for it to feel normal again. Happily the surgical wound healed well and caused no further problems, though it did leave a permanent hole in my skull behind the right ear. Fortunately, skin and hair covered it, so it was not easily visible.

Life returned to normal for a while, though punctuated by ever more goodbyes to friends and families we knew. The emigration diaspora, which had begun soon after the camps were established, was in full swing. In one week, three of my classmates left—for Canada, New Zealand, and Australia.

The outbound stream of émigrés continued, thinning out the population of young adults first. They were the immigrants all available countries preferred.

As we went on with everyday life, hoping something would break in our favor, it became harder for me to ignore the undercurrent of despair below the normalcy my parents so carefully maintained.

All camp activities went on as before, and the virtual normalcy bubble was maintained for us children. But I was almost ten now, and more aware of what the adults were doing and saying while trying to keep me in the dark.

The bubble was beginning to dissolve, even as I tried to bury my unease in books and pretend to be happy. My ability to get totally absorbed in novels was a saving grace.

One novel in particular had a deep impact. It was an adult literary classic called *Tõde ja Õigus* (Truth and Justice), about generations of two neighboring Estonian landholders with deep, complex, and often contentious relationships,

The philosophical and psychological themes in this book fascinated me even though I didn't understand the nuances. My resolve on the church steps during the war to figure out what life was all about resurfaced. I would have liked to discuss this book with my parents, but I had read it in secret because they would have said I was too young for it, so I couldn't. I settled for solitary brooding instead.

As 1948 rolled by and our ranks continued to thin with the ongoing migration to the far corners of the globe, life for us went on as usual, except there was nothing usual about it. We still hoped against hope that some country out there would accept us, but so far, no prospects.

A part of me was relieved. After three years, our apartment felt more and more like a real home, so I almost forgot it was temporary. There had been too many changes already, and this was an okay life as far as I was concerned.

Yet I also knew time was running out, with the end in sight. If we were still there when they closed the camp, would the Americans decide once more to hand us over to the Soviets? With friends and acquaintances leaving daily for far-away places, we were at a dead end.

No one seemed to want us. Why? There had to be a reason. I decided I was old enough to find out on my own.

Chapter 14

DEAD END

One day I walked by several older kids talking, and stopped. They might know something and be willing to tell me what was going on.

Throughout our camp life I had felt something ominous hovering around us, and knew that Soviet agents were trying to persuade people to return to occupied Estonia, but I could never get adults to talk to me about it. I was always told not to worry, that we were safe and would never go back.

After telling them about my unease, these young teens agreed to answer my questions as best they could.

What they told me was a shock. The relentless drive of the Soviet regime to capture and "repatriate" all refugees who had escaped from their conquered countries had never stopped. It had been in the background of my carefree life of school and play and pleasant family activities through all these years, and I never knew. After our narrow escape from Sarge and settling in Augsburg, I had almost forgotten that we were still stateless refugees.

It got worse. According to Tiina, the girl who was doing most of the talking, the Soviet agents were back, like vultures hoping that desperation would cause the DPs having trouble emigrating to be vulnerable to another "repatriation" pitch.

"They've been around," she explained, "bullying people with threats to their relatives in Estonia and lies that nothing would happen to them if they returned. It took several years for the Amis (Americans) to wise up to what the Russians were really doing to those they took 'home.' They had thought that being allies meant the Russians were okay, and therefore turned over people who flunked the interviews all adults had to go to."

"What interviews?" I was puzzled. "My parents never went to any interviews."

"Oh yes, they did," cut in Kalju, an older boy, with conviction. "Everyone had to meet personally with a Soviet agent accompanied by an American officer, to prove that they were not Soviet 'war criminals'."

"According to the Soviets, that would include us all just because we rejected their rule," Tiina added. "The trouble with the interviews was that they were in English, so people who didn't speak English often 'flunked' and were declared criminals by the NKVD guy."

That didn't make sense to me: "There are lots of people here who can translate."

"The Russians would not accept any translator who was Estonian because they were by definition unreliable, and would give answers to benefit their compatriots. That's what they said, which meant that there was almost no translation for anyone who didn't speak English. That made it easy for them to brand someone a war criminal."

Kalju's anger was all over his face.

"That's crazy." I couldn't believe what I was hearing.

"It's more than crazy. Many who were forced into Soviet custody committed suicide before they were taken, and those who were taken officially, or sometimes kidnapped, disappeared without a trace. After a while the suicides finally got the Amis' attention, so they stopped the interviews and turning over people who said they didn't want to go back. Better late than never."

Kalju's bitterness about the Americans' collusion made his voice shake. I suddenly remembered the violinist's suicide I had learned about from my parents a while back.

"So this is not happening anymore?" I asked, hoping.

"Well, not officially," Tiina explained, "but the Russkies try to twist people's arms anyway and play on their fears about the future. But now they mostly kidnap people they're really after when they go outside the camp, especially at night."

I felt a cold chill. What if my father had been kidnapped on his way to see me in the hospital every day? Were my parents stalked by the NKVD? How could I have known? I had been so clueless in my normalcy bubble, so well sheltered from everything they'd had to deal with.

I wasn't sure if I was upset about being left out or grateful for the protection. I was glad, though, to finally learn the truth. Now the grownups would have no reason to exclude me from their conversations. But they did anyway.

Despite being okay for as long as UNRRA continued to support us, watching so many others leave for their new homes—in Canada, Australia, New Zealand, England, the United States—left the rejects like us ever closer to despair.

Even Sweden was no longer an option, for their quotas were full and the rules had been tightened. In any case, because Sweden had turned over a number of Estonian refugees under heavy Soviet pressure, my parents were determined to go as far away from the Soviet threat as possible.

All things considered, our situation seemed pretty hopeless.

"Are you all right," Tiina asked, concerned about my long silence, "perhaps we told you too much?"

"No," I hastened to reply, "I'm glad you told me. It explains the weird feelings I've had that now make sense. I want to ask you another question too, since you've been nice enough to not treat me like a stupid child."

Tiina smiled tentatively, not sure what was coming.

"So many people have been accepted for emigration by different countries, and we have not," I continued. "My parents could work and take care of me and my sister just as well as the parents who have left. Why don't any of the countries want us?"

Tiina sighed. "I really don't know. We're having problems, too. That's why we're still here."

Kalju said he could guess. Older than the others at sixteen, he spoke with some authority. "I've heard people talk about the awful problems with immigration rules for different countries. All of them want young people eighteen or over who are healthy and can do physical labor. So they get picked first. Second, they want farm workers and domestic servants, preferably men and women with no children. There is little interest in artists and professionals. And none of them want the old or disabled. Old means fifty and over."

"Oh my gosh," I blurted out, "my father just had his fiftieth birthday. Could that be a reason?"

"It sure could," said Kalju.

"Don't you also have a grandmother with you," Tiina added. "which makes two unqualified people and two children, with only your mother considered employable. Or maybe not, since a mother of young children is not expected to get a job. I think you're all healthy, so not meeting all these stupid requirements is probably why they're rejecting you."

I was stunned. This made our ever finding a new home impossible. That is why my parents were talking about finding a sponsor as the only hope for us. A sponsor would be someone in a host country who was affluent enough to be responsible for us and guarantee our livelihood. We knew of no such person, and there was a very long list of people with a similar challenge.

Some religious groups did find sponsors for their congregants, but on a limited basis and with their own sets of rules, which had essentially the same restrictions. Only Jewish DPs were welcomed in Israel without any limitations.

Kalju told us that because of this strict selection process it was common for immigration to be offered to young adults alone without their aged parents, thus splitting up families. One member might be selected for Australia, another for Canada, while the parents were left behind to survive however they could.

Most elders would tell their children to go without them, but few agreed to leave their parents behind. That sometimes led to tragic outcomes. For example, a disabled father, whose daughters refused to leave him when offered emigration, hung himself when they were out of the house and left behind a loving note urging them to go and build a good life for themselves. When I heard this story, I almost burst out crying, but didn't want to in front of the older children.

Absorbing all this at once was becoming too much for me. I thanked Tiina, Kalju, and the other girl who had listened quietly but seemed sympathetic.

Holding back tears until I was out of sight, I realized that knowing the truth can be painful, and that is why my parents had worked so hard to keep it from me. But it was better than not knowing and living in a world that wasn't real.

Chapter 15

DEUS EX MACHINA

Life went on, but I was no longer happy. I kept praying that we wouldn't be abandoned in Germany with nowhere to go. It was clear the Germans didn't want us either.

Things looked hopeless. Even my parents were showing the stress on their faces despite heroic efforts to keep our bubble intact. For my little sister's sake, I tried too. Only four, she was now the only innocent one.

Then, one spring day in 1949 Father burst into the apartment after school looking jubilant, and, with uncharacteristic drama, announced: "We are going to America! A sponsor has been found!"

He and Mother were to go to the administrative office as soon as possible and fill out paperwork for immigration. Mother burst into tears, thoroughly confusing me.

"Why are you crying?" I asked. "I thought you want to go to America."

"Yes, of course," she smiled through her tears. "I am crying because I'm so happy."

Here was another adult reaction that didn't make sense to me. Neither did my own. I had hoped so fervently for this news so we could all stop worrying, but now I didn't know what I felt. I knew that we had to go live somewhere else because the camps would soon close, but this had become my home, my school was here, I had made friends.

Above all, I had mixed feelings about America from our earlier contacts with American soldiers, and even more after finding out recently that they had helped the Soviets and caused so much suffering to those sent back or committing suicide so they wouldn't have to. America was a dark unknown, so very far away from my real home in Tallinn, where I still hoped to return. Could we ever feel at home there?

Father was still jubilant: "Don't you want to know how this happened? I got a letter from a *saarlane* (man from Saaremaa, an island off the Estonian coast) in New York who arranged this miracle. It's quite a story."

Of course, we were all ears, so Father launched into relating in detail what a Mr. P had written in a letter addressed to him personally and passed on by an UNRRA functionary:

"Mr. P began by saying that he'd had to verify that I really am the son of 'Old Mart' for this to work. That's what the village people called my father. He was the schoolmaster and general resource for all kinds of information, from treating illnesses to agriculture to resolving conflicts. Sort of an all-purpose wise man. People trusted him.

"Well, there was a family with eight children who had trouble growing enough grain to last them through the winter, and Old Mart helped them every year, as he would anyone in need. I remembered when I read this letter that I sometimes helped him carry the bags of rye and honey. He was the only beekeeper on the island, and his honey was famous.

"I don't remember, but the letter says that one of their sons had come to America in the Thirties to make his fortune, and did. He is now wealthy, with a successful construction company in lower Manhattan and a nice house near New York on a long island. His second wife is from a wealthy American family who looks down on foreigners, so Gus, as he is called in America rather than August, isn't a regular part of the Estonian émigré community in New York. He only comes to Estonian House once in a while to touch base with his Saaremaa friends over beer and Estonian food.

"Mr.P, also an old-timer in New York, is one of the volunteers who are trying to help refugees, especially ones like us who have been rejected by the usual channels. In looking over the list of people seeking sponsorship, he thought he recognized my name and checked it out to see if I was from Saaremaa and related to Old Mart.

"He immediately thought of Gus, a rare prospect with enough resources to sponsor a family of five. When Gus happened to drop by for his periodic Estonian House meal, Mr. P brought out the list with our name on it. Gus scanned it half-heartedly to be polite, but was obviously not interested. Then, guess what?"

We waited for the punch line, which Father relished dragging out. I obliged by egging him on, "What? What? Tell us."

"Gus suddenly stopped in shock and asked, 'Is this Ruumet from Koimla Küla in Saaremaa?' 'He is Martin Ruumet's eldest son,' Mr. P answered. 'Is he someone you know?' No, said Gus, but he remembered that Old Mart used to help them through the winters when he was growing up, and since his father was too proud to accept charity, Old Mart was so clever about it that he couldn't refuse. Mart would bring bags of rye and some honey instead of the usual flowers or pastry as a traditional 'hostess gift' under the pretext of a routine visit to discuss how the kids were doing in school.

"Mr. P thought Gus looked misty-eyed when he described his mother secretly weeping in relief every time the old man dropped off his bags, and how he himself had looked forward to the honey. 'Get me the sponsorship papers,' were his next words.

"When Mr. P asked 'What will your wife say,' Gus said she wouldn't like it. She would say he was being a patsy, and who knows what kind of people these are, and he was an American now and didn't owe them anything. 'But this is something I have to do,' he concluded. Mr. P wrote that this surprised him, because Gus usually deferred to his wife, and so he wanted to personally relay the story to me so we would know how not only animosity but also good deeds can pass on through generations."

Mother and Mamma were weeping openly, Father's eyes were misty, and it suddenly hit me that I would probably never see my grandfather again. Somehow this had not sunk in earlier.

I remembered him vaguely from our summer visits. He had a beard and a strong, gentle presence, and he talked to me about bees. As a serious beekeeper, he was a novelty on the island, and his honey was coveted in the community. Our family took full advantage of this treat, and it was the first thing I asked for when we arrived at his farm for our summer visit.

What I most remembered was being stung by a bee when I was four years old, and his comforting me.

He explained that the bee didn't mean to hurt me. It got trapped inside a puffy sleeve on my dress and got so scared it tried to sting its way out. And because of that, the bee lost its stinger and no longer had a way of protecting itself, so the bee got hurt too.

That made me sad, and I though I'd better pay more attention in the future to not scaring them or letting them get trapped where they felt they had to sting. Although painful, the sting did not increase my fear of bees, just helped me understand them better.

My grandfather was such a kind man, not only to me but to everyone who visited while we were there. I would miss him so much, but it was better to think about that later. We had to focus on packing—and sailing to a whole new life.

It was exciting in a scary way. Everything would be new. I would not understand the language, or have friends I could talk to. But it would be an adventure.

Not knowing how to react to this radical news— however hoped for—I just let the jumble in my head rest as much as I could and hoped for the best. After all, everyone said America was a land where everyone was rich, lived in nice houses, and children had lots of toys.

Lots of books, too, I hoped.

Events moved quickly after that, and soon we were scheduled to sail for New York on a freighter converted to haul passengers: *Marine Marlin*, departing from Bremerhaven on May 1, 1949. The name of the ship was on my ticket, and it even had a passenger number: 320.

We retrieved the old suitcases we had arrived with four years earlier from the basement. They would have to hold all we could take to the other side of the world. Most of what we had lived with— furniture, lamps, dishes and utensils, even blankets and linens—did not belong to us, so those were to be cleaned and left for the next occupants.

Since the camp would have to be emptied of DPs within the next couple of years, new arrivals were unlikely, thus leaving the whole apartment to our co-residents, "Aunt Gertrude" and her son John. They were sad to see us go, and we to leave them behind. We had become like a family and their chances to emigrate with Gertrude's disability were slim. That meant John would stay, too. His father had been lost in the war, and he would take care of his mother no matter what.

My parents promised that once we got to America we would do what we could to help them follow us. It was a promise they kept.

For me, leaving my remaining friends in Augsburg was the hardest part. It was unlikely we would ever see each other again. Their future was unknown and we would probably end up in different parts of the world. Would I ever again have so many friends close by to have fun with? I doubted it. But I had always known this was never meant to be permanent. I was beginning to think nothing was.

I didn't mind going by ship. I loved ships and never got seasick.

Mother had told me when I was very little and we were bouncing around on a boat to Saaremaa, that our seafaring ancestors going back 300 years that we knew of didn't ever get seasick, so neither would we. I believed her, and never did. That made crossing the ocean fun, though it took much longer than I had expected. I never imagined there could be so much water anywhere.

During the voyage, Mother coached me in saying some English words required to be polite: Yes and No, Please and Thank You/No Thank You, Hello and Goodbye. With what little I had learned in our camp school from reading a couple of short children's stories in English, it was a start.

After what seemed like forever, we approached New York harbor on May 9, 1949. Sailing past the Statue of Liberty was thrilling. I was awed as she loomed before us in all her majesty, growing in size as we got closer. Since we did not have to go through Ellis Island, our ship headed straight to a dock on Manhattan's West Side, where "Uncle Gus" would be waiting to greet us.

I wondered what he would be like. I had already decided that he had to be wonderful because he was the hero who had appeared out of nowhere to save us.

By now the sea air had cleared my qualms, and on this sunlit May morning I was open to giving America a chance. Maybe it really could become our home. Excited in spite of myself, and with a surging case of stage fright, I waved to Lady Liberty and whispered: "Hello, America."

PART II
DELIVERANCE

Chapter 16

HELLO LADY LIBERTY

As we slowly made our way through the mouth of the Hudson River toward a dock on Manhattan's West side, the view of skyscrapers had us blinking in wonder. A huge urban forest slowly emerged one tower at a time, unveiling canyons of narrow streets in-between. These first images of America took my breath away.

Once docked, we scrambled to get our belongings together for debarking. Solid ground felt strange after getting used to balancing on a swaying deck.

I was giddy with excitement about arriving on this new continent. The ocean had seemed endless and America had seemed a magical far-away place, like a fairy tale. That it would now be our home, and that we were actually there, felt unreal.

The dock was a maelstrom of multilingual humanity, the new arrivals scanning for familiar faces, or simply trying to locate a space to sit down and wait to be found. My parents were directed to an office to do paperwork and hopefully connect with our sponsor, while Mamma stayed with my now four-year-old sister and me to wait with the luggage.

This time I was not scared as I watched them wend their way through the crowd and disappear from view. It felt safe to be in America. But what a crowded, chaotic place it was.

Mamma, wearing her favorite navy dress, sat on the biggest suitcase with her back ramrod-straight, planted her feet squarely on the ground and hugged her weathered brown leather purse to her body in a protective grip. It held her precious family photographs, her worn Bible, several books from Estonia, and her handicraft tools.

For a woman almost seventy years old, she appeared confident and far from frail, but to my eyes she looked pale and nervous. I had never seen her like that before. She had always been actively engaged or in charge of any task at hand, but now she looked lost.

Her assertive pose did not fool me. For the first time in her life, although fluent in three languages, she didn't understand a word spoken around her, and would now have to depend on her children. She would hate that.

Mamma had been responsible for other people from an early age. As the oldest of thirteen children, she quickly became mother's helper as her string of siblings grew. Although they had household help, her mother could not keep track of everyone. Luckily, they lived in a close-knit village where children roamed freely from home to home.

She once told us there were times when, rather than tracking everyone down one by one at dinner-time, mothers simply counted their usual number of children, sat them at the table, and shut the door. If some diners belonged to other people, fine. Their own missing ones would get fed somewhere else.

Mamma spoke of her childhood with nostalgia, as happy and very busy. She enjoyed having work to do.

Her parents had a romantic story of their own that I loved to hear. Her father was a Swedish merchant who had come to the north coast of Estonia and bought fourteen hectares of land in Võsu, a coastal resort village, where he built a number of vacation cottages for city folk. Rumor had it that he got embroiled with the king somehow and was banished, but no one knew if it was true.

He fell in love with the daughter of a high-ranking Prussian officer living in Estonia, who defied her parents to marry him. For that, her father disowned her and never spoke to her again. In his world, a Swedish merchant, however prosperous, was not a suitable addition to his aristocratic family.

Neither Mamma nor her siblings ever met either grandparent, nor were they acknowledged by them in any way.

In spite of this, Mamma's parents were happy together, and her mother became much loved in the area as an herbalist and healer. Mother remembered that in response to someone coming to the door, she would put on her black wool cape, grab her black medicine bag and go off day or night to tend someone sick.

She died from an illness contracted from one of her patients, leaving Mamma as virtual mother to her siblings.

In her late twenties and facing a future as an "old maid," Mamma married a widower from neighboring Käsmu village, called "Captains' Village" because it was the ancestral home of seafaring families who had owned and sailed ships across the globe for several centuries.

Tragically, their marriage was short. When my mother, their first and only child, was a year old, her father drowned under mysterious circumstances next to his own ship in Tallinn Harbor, and she would never know him. That such an experienced sea captain could fall off his own ship and drown generated murmurings of foul play, but the mystery of his death was never solved.

This tragedy left Mamma on her own. She was expected to stay in her husband's house, raise their child, and receive financial support from his ship's revenues. His relatives would appoint a new captain for the ship and take charge of her finances.

They didn't know whom they were dealing with. Mamma insisted that one of her own brothers, though less experienced than their choice, captain the ship. The result was an impasse. Holding the financial power, her husband's relatives prevailed.

Mamma felt wronged, and deference was not in her nature. She took her baby and left, knowing she was giving up the house and the support that would have been hers.

She decided to raise her daughter on her own—
no small task for a widow trained neither as a teacher
nor a nurse, the only respectable professions in the
early 20th Century that could provide a decent living
for women. Surprisingly, after a brief return to her
family, she got a job on a baronial estate in the same
region.

She became the head housekeeper in charge of the
estate when the Baron and his family were absent,
and turned out to be well suited for the job. Mother
told me that other staff had described Mamma as a
fair but effective boss who ran a tight ship.

Her childhood image of Mamma had her walking
around with a big ring of keys around her waist, dis-
pensing supplies and giving orders to the cook, indoor maids, and outdoor staff. She had seemed very
comfortable in that role. Thus it was not surprising
now to see her sitting with mock bravado on a bat-
tered suitcase on a foreign dock, where nothing at all
was familiar.

Worst of all, there was nothing for her to *do*.

Finally my parents reappeared, accompanied by
a tall, handsome man wearing a light gray suit and
a big smile, who welcomed us with gusto. As I had
expected, I liked him immediately. I was not used to
the public display of exuberance, but I liked that too.

Uncle Gus, as he asked to be called, grabbed two
of our suitcases and led us out of the crowd along a
street lined with cars, to a large Cadillac squeezed
between two smaller cars. To my eyes, it was huge.
I had never seen a car that big. It looked almost like
a boat.

We didn't drive long before pulling up in front of a hotel. Uncle Gus led us straight through the lobby into an elevator. We got off on the sixth floor. He already had a key.

The room was large, with a double bed, a twin, and a cot. This would be our home until an apartment could be found and Father had gotten a job.

He told us to rest, get acquainted with the neighborhood, and enjoy what Manhattan had to offer. There was much to see, and so many points of interest were easily accessible, especially the big park down the street called Central Park, with a playground and even a zoo nearby.

If my parents wanted to take a longer walk, there was a famous art museum farther uptown on Fifth Avenue. He gave us a street map of Manhattan marked with our location and where to find food stores as well as the places he had described.

He would pay all our expenses until we could make it on our own, and as soon as we were settled, he would take us to his house on Long Island to meet his family. Before he left, he took us to a neighborhood restaurant for a good meal. Starry-eyed, I decided I was going to like America—a lot.

Our room at the hotel was furnished with a small icebox and some basic utensils provided by him, making it possible to put together simple meals in the room.

Otherwise, there were delis and coffee shops nearby, as well as the Automat, a New York establishment that fascinated me. You put coins into what looked like postal boxes with glass doors, and took out a plate with whatever you chose from soup to my favorite, lemon meringue pie. It became my favorite place to eat, much more fun than a restaurant.

Having a modern bathroom all to ourselves, with round-the-clock hot water, was wonderful.

Getting used to the constant level of big-city noise was hard, though. Uncle Gus had warned us that New York was known as "the city that never sleeps," and he was right.

Traffic sounds went on all night, punctuated by police and ambulance sirens, and from our room, the additional clunk and hiss of the elevator when tourists came in from their nights on the town. We would have to develop the ability to tune out background noises, but our ears were still in shock. Falling and staying asleep was a challenge.

There was even more noise in the daytime, the city flooding all the senses: so much to look at, new foods and beverages to taste, the constant traffic and human activity, and so many diverse smells, especially on garbage collection days. It was exciting. And overwhelming.

Those first two weeks, living several blocks from the park with easy access to everything in Manhattan, was a dream come true, especially after getting acquainted with the subway and buses.

For my sister and me, the most important stop during our outings was the Good Humor man's cart at the entrance to Central Park with its chocolate-coated ice cream bars. We took full advantage of the playground swings and climbing equipment, and especially Central Park Zoo with the infamous gorilla known for randomly and accurately spitting at people standing in front of his cage.

We fed the ever-present pigeons our leftover bread crusts, and had picnics on the grass with Mamma while Mother and Father were off on their errands.

It was so much fun I didn't ever want to leave this place, but I knew we would have to. As always. But maybe that would mean having a real home just as nice, where we could settle down and I could find friends again.

After two weeks in Manhattan, we did move. The nice Mr. P who had alerted Uncle Gus to our emigration predicament had found Father a job as a building superintendent in the upper Bronx, a short distance from Van Cortland Park. A free two-bedroom apartment in the basement came with the job, a welcome perk for our family of five.

Father, of course, had no experience to qualify him for the job, but Mr. P had managed to sell the idea to the owner anyway, banking on Father being smart enough to fake it while he learned the ropes.

Since my parents were embarrassed about depending on Uncle Gus's generosity, and the apartment made the super's salary sufficient to meet our basic needs, we were grateful to find a way to be self-sufficient so quickly. Or so we hoped, if Father could master the job fast enough.

Chapter 17

FROM CLASSROOM TO BOILER ROOM

Our new location was a letdown after Manhattan. It was an ordinary street of nondescript five and six-story apartment buildings, ours U-shaped with an entry courtyard leading to the front door and elevator lobby, and two wings of apartments on either side.

The street was nothing but grey concrete and parked cars, pleasant enough but in dire need of some trees and plants.

The entry to our apartment was ugly — a descending concrete ramp down a passageway from the street to basement level, with garbage containers to the left as we reached the bottom. The basement door to the right led past a black painted door with a big white sign, "Boiler Room," that you couldn't miss.

A dim hallway led to the elevator and storage areas beyond.

To the left, an empty space with numerous concrete columns with a strangely random placement pattern ended at the door to our apartment. They made the whole basement feel dreary and oppressive.

Father said their purpose was to support the building, but the prospect of my beauty-loving mother living there still made me sad.

The apartment itself, however, turned out to be
surprisingly clean and roomy. It took up the back
corner of the building, making it possible to have
windows in every room. The bedrooms and living
room faced the back of the building, kitchen and
bathroom the side. Though all you could see through
the windows was a six-foot chain-link fence and the
rear of other similar buildings, the apartment did get
adequate light.

The back "yard" was paved concrete, totally bare.
No plants of any kind there, either. But I was sure
Mother and Mamma would soon make some nice
curtains to mask the view and find potted plants to
cheer up the space.

The inside was clean, with furniture in every room.
That was a lovely surprise. It seems Mr. P had been
busy putting this together for us while we were at the
hotel. The dark wooden kitchen table and chairs had
been donated by a charity, along with a chest of draw-
ers and chair for each bedroom. The living room had a
plain but clean sofa and armchair of a brownish color,
blending with a weathered wood coffee table.

There were enough beds for everyone in the two
bedrooms, and these were new. Uncle Gus wanted
us to have fresh, clean bedding, so he had bought
those himself. Kitchen utensils were eclectic, but the
necessities were there and usable.

I knew Mother would find a way to make this
space homey, and once Mamma, our Kitchen Queen,

got her moxie back, there would be delicious smells greeting us when we entered the apartment, especially if she decided to bake fresh bread again. All in all, with some creativity and hard work, the apartment would be fine.

Our part was easy compared to Father's. He was now the superintendent of a five-story building full of people expecting heat and hot water every day, but neither of my parents had ever laid eyes on a boiler before. It was the centerpiece of the basement—without it, no heat, no hot water.

With some trepidation, and Mr. P as their guide, they went to meet The Big Black Boiler. They discovered it to be a floor-to-ceiling, giant variant of a potbellied stove with a huge fire-filled maw into which the piles of coal along the wall had to be shoveled on a regular feeding schedule.

That part was simple physical labor. The tricky part was to get it going every morning. Mr. P, who had been the head super of a large apartment building for many years, provided directions that seemed easy enough—until the next morning when my parents tried it without him. The boiler sat there in stony silence, indifferent to their efforts and prayers. Nothing they tried worked.

Meanwhile, all the people upstairs would soon be getting up expecting to take a warm shower. Father was embarrassed to call Mr. P so early, but he was desperate. Fortunately, the apartment came with a working telephone.

His frantic SOS brought our generous benefactor rushing back to intercede with the Boiler Genie, who now graciously responded. I guess Father proved acceptable to the Genie after that, because from then on the morning ritual worked, and heat flowed with no further glitches.

The custodial work was not a problem. Father had grown up on a farm and knew how to wield a scythe. He had enjoyed harvesting hay on his father's farm when he was on summer vacation. That he tended to wield the broom like a scythe must have looked peculiar to the tenants, but it got the job done.

He was meticulous in everything he did, and that carried over to this new occupation. The condition of the building, as well as the sidewalk which he swept daily, pleased the tenants and assured that he was in no immediate danger of being fired as an impostor. That helped us all to relax.

Something puzzled my parents, though. They couldn't understand why a number of residents were distant and almost unfriendly toward us for no apparent reason. In view of the feedback that Father was doing a good job, this didn't make sense.

It took a number of weeks and Mother's improving English to unravel the mystery. When she heard us referred to as "German" during a conversation, she discovered that when we arrived, the tenant grapevine had us coming from Germany, so they had assumed we were German.

Mother was surprised, and explained that we were not; we were Estonian refugees who had come to America to escape both Russians and Germans. We had no homeland to return to. She then realized that since many of the tenants were Jewish, it had been difficult for them to welcome what they thought was a German family into their midst. It was good to clarify the facts.

Some tenants were still skeptical, however. Several retired women in the building decided to test us. They reasoned that if my mother were telling the truth, my sister and I probably wouldn't understand German even if our multilingual elders did.

So they would unexpectedly say something to us in German that a child would naturally respond to, and then watch our response. My sister, now four, looked totally blank when addressed in German, while I tried to come up with a response, but my awkwardness was obvious. I had forgotten almost all the German I had learned.

They also eavesdropped on our conversations in Estonian, a language akin to Finnish and ancient Hungarian that bears no resemblance to German. Finally they were convinced, and word got around.

From then on everyone was nice to us. Mamma could even communicate with some of the tenants through a German-Yiddish amalgam embellished by improvised sign language. That generated some understanding and even camaraderie.

Her strategy also helped with neighborhood shopkeepers, especially her favorite butcher. She was quite particular about how her meat was cut, and her expertise earned his respect. He sometimes even asked how she would cut a piece for a particular purpose.

He never knew, of course, that it came from having run an estate that had grown, butchered, and prepared its own meat.

My father's work ethic soon earned the respect of the previously suspicious women, the self-appointed social arbiters of the building, who soon guessed that he was not a "real" super. When Mr. P visited, they must have pumped him for information, because they started referring to Father as "The Professor."

Sometimes they kibitzed on his attempts to fix plumbing or other mechanical problems, politely sharing how they had seen the former super do it. Father's own approach was to figure out theoretically how the thing should work and then test various possible methods until something did.

Fortunately the ladies' genuine helpfulness often shortened the experiments.

Mother laughingly teased him about his coterie of "lady friends," but their friendliness was genuine. It would have taken only a couple of complaints to the owners to get him fired as a fake, but none ever came—only praise, which Mother figured was more a tribute to him as a person than his mastery of the job.

By the time we left a year and a half later he had learned enough to be a credible super, and he held on to his union card for several years afterward just in case.

During our Bronx era, I accomplished two things: learning English to basic fluency, and learning to roller skate on the streets. With an English-Estonian dictionary by my side, I devoured Nancy Drew mystery books as the main vehicle for learning the language quickly.

Before our first summer I had only several weeks in fifth grade before the break, barely enough time to meet and befriend several girls on my street. My frustration at not being able to communicate adequately sparked a determination to know enough English by September to not be thought stupid by other students just because I did not understand their language. That had been my experience during the brief time in school before summer vacation.

I wondered why Americans seemed to equate not speaking English with lack of intelligence, and why they raised their voices when not understood the first time, as though strange sounds would be easier to decipher when shouted.

Though most of them were not mean, other children and even adults often talked to me as though I were a three-year-old, which was insulting but also a powerful incentive.

My grades in all language-dependent subjects soared during the following school year. Math had been a breeze all along, which fortunately signaled to the teachers that I was not the dummy other kids thought I was. But I was more focused on being respected by my peers.

During that year, I was also introduced to television. My first new friend Roberta lived in the building next to ours, and her family had a television. Seeing it for the first time was magical.

They invited me often to watch *Howdy Doody*, *Mickey Mouse*, and *The Ed Sullivan Show*. I also listened to the radio a lot, *The Lone Ranger* and *The Shadow* mystery series being my favorites, but nothing on radio could compare with the magic box with a little movie screen. I couldn't wait for us to have one too.

I loved the emotional expressiveness and open displays of affection in Roberta's family: the way her father would nuzzle her mother while she was cooking, and sometimes pat her bottom as he passed.

At other times, they would openly argue, gesticulating with raised voices and following each other from room to room, only to kiss and make up five minutes later. I had never seen anything like that at home and, like Uncle Gus's exuberance, I liked it.

I wanted to be more like that when I grew up, and have a family where we would express our emotions freely. I enjoyed learning about different ways of being, and soon concluded it might be possible for me to feel at home in this new country after all.

I liked the people I had met so far, and the more English I learned the easier it became to have a real conversation.

Chapter 18

CULTURE GAP WITH MISS GRUNDY

In the sweltering August heat of New York, even the concrete buildings and sidewalks oozed heat and sweat through the night, keeping us groggy through the even hotter days.

Our family had experienced nothing like that before. As we were wilting away, an Estonian-American man called and asked if my parents would like to send me to the country for a week. He worked with a Lutheran relief organization that placed "Fresh Air Children" from New York City—poor children who otherwise had no access to the great outdoors—for a week's "fostering" with families on Long Island.

He saw it as a great opportunity for me to see a more typical face of America. I would learn more English and get to know my new country better.

I had just turned eleven, and my parents left the decision up to me. We had only recently arrived and it meant going away from family to another unknown place. That felt intimidating. But my curiosity won out and, with some trepidation, I decided to go.

Mr. T was a jolly, portly middle-aged father of several children and seemed to genuinely like all children. With three or four other fresh air seekers in the hot car, we drove out to a small town on Long Island, a pleasant place with a lot of greenery, large well-kept yards with picket fences, and two-story wooden houses that reminded me of my early life in suburban Tallinn.

I was dropped off at a white house with a white picket fence, home to an elderly woman whose appearance reminded me of "Miss Grundy," the prune-faced, stern teacher from the Archie comic books I had recently been devouring. That became my secret name for her.

She lived alone. The interior had a musty Victorian feel, with lace doilies, highly polished walnut furniture, and worn oriental rugs.

She looked me over from head to foot and welcomed me with a big smile. She seemed nice, but something about her felt false. Her smile showed a lot of teeth but her eyes were not smiling, and her manner was brusque with a forced cheery overlay.

When Mr. T had left, she led me up a staircase, not noticing that I paused on the landing to put my suitcase down for a moment. It was too heavy for me. She didn't slow down or look around, so I struggled after her and caught up just in time to enter the bedroom that would be mine for the week.

It was very clean, with two twin beds, a bureau, and an antique armoire, which I was to use for my belongings.

"Go ahead and hang up your clothes so the wrinkles hang out. When you are done, come down. I will be in the kitchen," she said, never looking at me. Then she left.

I felt a bit queasy, and wished I hadn't come, but reminded myself that she was being generous. Hadn't I learned that people are not always the way they look on the outside? And didn't the Girl Scouts' camp in Germany turn out so much better than expected, especially with the quarantine afterward? Besides, I was pretty much trapped here for a week, so why not try to please her?

When I went downstairs, she was preparing dinner and asked me to set the table for the two of us. She showed me where the china and utensils were, with no further instructions.

It was nice china, and I remembered with a twinge that right before leaving Estonia, Mother had buried her china and much of her silverware near the farmhouse we had rented for that last summer. We had expected to return after the war was over, and she would have known where to find it again. That twinge of pain in my stomach always came when something reminded me of my earliest years.

I centered the plates between the crochet edges of the place mats and, as I had always seen Mamma and Mother do, placed the utensils on the right and the folded napkins on the left. I thought it looked pretty.

When Miss Grundy came to look, she tsk-tsk'ed in a deliberate, sweetly patronizing tone: "Well, I see you have not been taught how to set the table properly. We'll have to take care of that, won't we?"

"This is the way my mother does it," I responded defensively.

"I'm sure she does, dear," she smirked, "but we'll make sure you know the right way by the time you leave."

She has no right to insult my parents like that, I thought, and hated her calling me "dear." But I remembered that children should not talk back to adults.

Dinner was awkward and silent. I focused on holding back the tears that were welling up. I helped her dry the dishes and put them away, not knowing what to say.

It was a relief when bedtime came, and I had no problem accepting the early hour she had decided was appropriate. Maybe I could find something to read that would take my mind off the disappointment and humiliation I felt. I did not sleep well that night, even though it was much cooler than in the city.

The week also had a bright side. I loved being out in her garden, especially a glider in the shade of a massive tree where I liked to curl up and smell the fragrance of the flowers—as well as the fresh air I had been sent there to enjoy.

I wondered why she seemed offended whenever I explored the garden by myself, and once when I tried to read a book I had finally found that interested me, she snapped that we had better things to do, like my helping her. I would have if asked.

It turned out that meant going food shopping with her, and being introduced to her friends in town

as her "fresh air child." Her way of saying it suggested what a boon it was for a poor urchin like me to be
staying with her, and her patronizing tone annoyed
me.

Nevertheless, I curtsied and said hello when introduced, though it surprised me that no one initiated a
handshake. That seemed unfriendly. I felt awkward
and alien, being ignorant of the differences between
social niceties in America versus Europe.

The saving grace was group activities every afternoon for us visiting children. About the fifth day, the
local minister and his wife invited Miss Grundy and
me to lunch, with several other children and their
hosts.

The gathering seemed pleasant, the food was
good, and Miss Grundy was smiling and talking
with great animation in a way I had not seen before.
I wondered if that was her real personality, and if I
was somehow the one making her grouchy.

When the adult conversation turned to the fresh
air program and its benefits, I heard her say, in response to praise heaped on the minister for promot-
ing it:

"It is well and good to get these poor children out
of those horrible slums. They certainly need fresh air
and healthy food. But I think it is even more important that we give them the opportunity to learn some
proper manners in a civilized home."

Hearing that, I had an impulse to throw something at her and felt a wave of hot anger rising. I did
not live in a slum, and my parents had better manners than what I'd seen her display.

It was hard to sit there and say nothing. They talked about us children as though we were either deaf or too stupid to understand what they were saying. Or was Miss Grundy purposely trying to insult me because I didn't fit her expectations, whatever they were?

I didn't hear how the minister or the others responded, because I was too focused on controlling myself. I was determined not to validate Miss Grundy's prejudices by acting "uncivilized."

When lunch was finally over and we were saying goodbye, I stood quietly while Miss Grundy thanked our hosts, and curtsied modestly when they said goodbye to me. I responded with a smile when they said how delighted they were to have met me.

That was how I had been taught to behave. Children in the Europe I knew, when in adult company, stayed quietly in the background, responded when asked a question, and curtsied (or bowed, if boys) when shaking hands hello or goodbye.

A child never extended a hand or spoke first, and since in America, women did not shake hands at all as far as I had seen, I decided to still curtsy as a show of respect. I thought the evening had gone well, in spite of Miss Grundy's comments, and I liked the minister and his wife.

On the drive home, from the moment we left the others and got in the car, Miss Grundy sat in tight-lipped silence, exuding disapproval. I had no clue what her problem was, but when we got into the house, she exploded with a shrillness that shocked and frightened me:

"How can you embarrass me like that? Have your parents never taught you any manners? You stood there like an idiot and didn't even say thank you to the Reverend when we left. And you never even tried to be friendly to anyone at the table. I know you haven't been taught much, but couldn't you *try?*"

I was so shaken by her insult to my parents, and so shocked by her tirade, that I burst into tears, repeating "I want to go home!" several times as I ran upstairs to my room.

When she followed a few minutes later and knocked on the door, I told her, "Call Mr. T and ask him to take me home."

When she asked if she could come in I said no. She accepted my refusal and left, for which I was grateful.

I started folding my clothes and packing. Nothing could make me stay there any longer. She tried again about ten minutes later, and I just kept repeating, "Call Mr. T. I want to go home. I don't want to stay here."

Tears flowed until I fell into an exhausted sleep.

Several hours later, Mr. T knocked on my door and asked to come in. I was so relieved to see him, and after hearing my story he realized I was absolutely set on going home. He said okay, took my suitcase, and we went downstairs.

Miss Grundy, seeming surprised that he had not changed my mind, realized we were really leaving. "Are you sure, dear?" she asked with saccharine sweetness.

I didn't even look at her, just said "Yes." I was not her "dear," I fumed inwardly.

Remembering my manners, I added, "Thank you for my nice room and good food."

That was all I could honestly thank her for, but now she couldn't say I didn't know how to say "thank you."

As we walked out the door and Mr. T said, "I'm sorry it didn't work out for you two," she sighed. "Well, these poor children are emotionally damaged, but we do the best we can, don't we?"

That undid any remnants of good feeling I had toward her. Since this had been my first immersion in what I'd heard referred to as the "real America," in contrast to New York, the world's "melting pot," I felt queasy in my stomach as something inside me shouted: "You don't belong here." I had come with high hopes, but for the rest of the summer, the fresh air in Van Cortland Park would be enough for me, and I would stay with the people I understood who accepted me as I was.

My adventurous spirit crushed, I stayed close to home and played with Roberta, whose family was so different from what I had just experienced—thank goodness. My brain tried to make sense of what had happened, but there were too many contradictions.

I spent long blocks of time through the rest of the summer entertaining myself with Nancy Drew mysteries, comic books, and magazines I found in our basement's throwaway pile, and gave up trying to understand grownups, especially Americans.

Yet Miss Grundy had left a wound in my heart that still hurt.

Chapter 19

BROOKLYN

Our move to Brooklyn in 1950 when I was in the sixth grade was the beginning of our family's "normal" life in America.

An estimator's job had opened up in Uncle Gus's construction office, and he asked if Father would be interested. He was delighted. Though knowing little about the construction business, his mathematical skills would be put to use, and he could quickly learn the rest. As a bonus, his meager English would not be a barrier because several of the top staff spoke Estonian.

Mother had already found a clerical job at First National City Bank's main office in lower Manhattan, so Father's new job, also in lower Manhattan, would shorten the commute for them both, especially from our new location.

How they found this particular apartment in the middle of Brooklyn, so far from where we had lived, I couldn't imagine, but I liked it.

It was a "railroad apartment," New Yorkese for a long apartment typical of narrow townhouses, characterized by a sequence of rooms strung along one side of a long corridor except when it passed right through a room.

Ours had an L-shaped living room facing the street, then a hallway passing the master bedroom, a bath, a second bedroom, and a walk-through wood-paneled dining room with built-in glass-front cabinets. A kitchen and then a smaller bedroom facing the rear of the building followed, with a nice view of green back yards and a church steeple a block away.

Originally intended as a maid's room, the back room also had a tiny adjoining bathroom and served Mamma's need for a private space of her own, right next to her kitchen.

With both parents at work all day, Mamma's presence was essential for the family to function. She held down the home front, was there when my sister and I came home from school, and had a delicious dinner ready at six thirty every night. To the whole family, she was our undisputed Kitchen Queen. That took a big burden off Mother's shoulders.

Schooling posed a new challenge, especially now that my sister was ready for first grade. The elementary school in our new district was some distance away, so Father somehow convinced the principal of a Catholic school down the block to admit us even though we were not Roman Catholic. The tuition was a stretch but he was determined that our education take precedence over other expenses.

The only condition set by the school was that I had to do well in my studies and attend Mass every Sunday, as well as receive religious instruction like everyone else. Although Mamma, a devout Lutheran, expressed misgivings, my parents had no objection. They thought learning more about Catholicism would broaden my education.

Besides, Father had a soft spot in his heart for nuns. During his wartime flight from the Russians toward the West, at a crucial moment when he was on the verge of getting caught, they had hidden him inside their convent. He playfully bragged that he was the only man he could think of who had spent two weeks of his life under a nun's bed.

He also gratefully remembered the nuns who had cared for me in the midst of the war, when I was sick and Mother was giving birth.

Now I was once more in the care of nuns, but this time I welcomed it. I expected them to be nice, and they were. That was not always so for some of the boys in the class who did not toe the line, and I did not want to share the experience of a boisterous boy named Tony who often spent time on his knees in the corner, so I was careful to behave.

I also knew I was an outsider and therefore on probation. The priest who agreed to accept my sister and me had made that very clear.

Both of us did well. She was such a sweet child that it couldn't have been otherwise, and I was determined to make my parents proud. It was also important for me to prove that I was as smart as any of the American kids, even though I was starting from behind.

My English was good by then, but this school was academically almost a year ahead of my former

school, so I spent the first few months working hard
to catch up. After that, I could complete my homework quickly and have time for my own interests, as
well as attending the newly created cultural enrichment school every other Saturday that my father had
helped establish at Estonian House.

Since I had already attended an Estonian school
in the DP camp, I didn't feel I needed any further
enrichment, but Father, as the principal, insisted that
his own children set an example and attend. It was
a command performance I complied with but did
not like—until a cute boy who sparked my interest
joined the class. That tipped the scales.

Every trip to Manhattan took about forty-five
minutes each way on the subway, with Father and I
both absorbed in books we had brought along. It was
a nice time together even if not much was said. It was
too noisy to have a conversation anyway.

As I grew into my teens and Estonian House became the hub of my social life, New York's subways
became, for all practical purposes, my study hall. Giv-
en how much time I spent traveling underground, it
was where I got most of my homework done.

During eighth grade, since the local public high
school was said to have problems with gangs and
drugs, both my parents and teachers encouraged me
to take the admission test for Hunter High School,
an elite public school with high academic standards,
located in Manhattan and a long subway ride away. I
was admitted, and resigned myself to the daily grind
of long subway rides like the ones I was already used
to on weekends, but things took an unexpected turn.

One day my teacher pulled me aside in the hall-way. She told me that a private girls' academy in Brooklyn was offering two full four-year scholar-ships on the basis of a competitive exam, and that I should go and take the test the following Saturday.

"I think you have a chance to win," she said, "and this is a terrific opportunity."

"I don't see how I could possibly win," I replied, "and there's something else I'm supposed to do this Saturday."

I thought it would be a total waste of time, and I'd rather be with my friends. She looked disappointed, then drew herself up to her full height, looked me in the eye, and said emphatically:

"I am telling you to go and take that test. If you don't, don't bother coming to school on Monday."

Wow, I didn't expect that.

"Yes, Sister," I responded meekly, still thinking it a waste of time, but I clearly had no choice.

On Saturday I navigated the bus system to the school, an imposing gray stone building, and took a lengthy multiple-choice test culminating in a short written essay. Having fulfilled my commit-ment, I went on to Estonian House and joined my friends.

That evening, when I went home, Mother told me she had run into several of my classmates who excit-edly told her something about me and a scholarship test. It sounded as if I had won, but she wasn't sure. I assured her she had misunderstood. It must have been a prank, and I didn't think it was nice of them to involve my mother.

The next morning at Mass, I sat daydreaming as usual while the ritual was running its course when I heard a voice from the pulpit, as if from a great distance:

"And we are happy to announce that one of our eighth-graders, Hillevi Ruumet, has been awarded a full scholarship to attend Saint Angela Hall Academy next year."

I was so shocked I nearly fell off the pew. I felt a hundred eyes on me, including the priest who smiled and added, "We are all very proud of you, Hillevi. Congratulations."

I barely managed a smile and a thank you. It felt like a dream and everything was happening in slow motion. Was it real? I had hurried through the test, not even nervous because I didn't take it seriously and was in a hurry to finish. How could I possibly have won?

When my teacher came to congratulate me after Mass, I asked her: "Are you sure? What about my not being Catholic? Do they know that?"

She smiled and looked very pleased with herself:

"Yes they do. Once they let you take the test, they agreed to abide by the results, and yours was one of the two top scores."

It was then that I realized her role in this. She must have talked them into letting me compete. No wonder she had been so adamant.

I was still in shock on the way home, and couldn't wait to tell my parents. They would be thrilled. Maybe angels did work through humans when needed, even when we acted as stupidly as I would have if

Sister hadn't forced the issue.

Maybe she was their instrument, I thought, although I couldn't imagine angels acting so bossy.

Chapter 20

BULLIED INTO EXCELLENCE

The Sisters of Saint Joseph, our teachers at St. Angela Hall, were all different under their black habits and starched white wimples—lively, quiet, humorous, serious, practical, visionary, playful.

Even sanctimonious, like Sister Calasanctius. That really was her name. She taught religion and I never saw her crack a smile. Hers was a serious, no-nonsense classroom, focused on dogma, sin, and the dubiousness of salvation for any of us who misbehaved.

In stark contrast, the frail, rapidly aging Sister Manuella, our other religion teacher, did not walk but glided through the halls with a beatific expression, slipping ever farther from this everyday world, her wimple off-center at a jaunty angle and a beneficent smile on her face. She could see no evil, and thought of us all as sweet angels. In gratitude, we tried not to disillusion her.

What all the nuns had in common was a mastery of "tough love," the essence of discipline that governed all our activities from dress code and conduct to academic rigor. Some of the firm structure was enforced quite gently, some with humor, and some with neither, but the consequences of detected infractions were inexorable.

Hence we all tried to appear as "good" as possible. Since many of the rules seemed silly, however, we couldn't help pushing the envelope just for the fun of it.

The dress code was a particularly fertile field. Since the school's goal, second in importance only to college preparation, was to turn us into proper young ladies with all the necessary social graces, we not only had to wear a uniform to school, but also nylon stockings and black pumps, a white beret that came off only indoors, white gloves—and no makeup.

That made red M&M's valued contraband, since they stained enough to give our lips a bit of color while providing truthful deniability.

"Young lady, are you wearing lipstick?"

"No, Sister."

"Then why are your lips so red?"

"I don't know. Maybe some red candy I ate."

Said with a look of wide-eyed innocence, it was usually enough, and by the letter of the law it was the truth. They probably knew the game we were playing, but we thought we were pretty clever.

Hats were another issue. The requirement was to wear them all the way to and from school, or demerits would follow. We felt conspicuous enough on the bus or subway with our uniform, pumps, and stockings.

The challenge became to see how close to the school we could get before plopping the hated beret on our heads. Since the nuns could see us through the windows, and a few sometimes took an early morning walk in the neighborhood, there was always the prospect of getting caught. The risk made it interesting.

We were also to go straight home after school and not linger in the neighborhood, especially in soda shops or restaurants. We saw this prohibition as extreme.

For me, rebellion was motivated by pizza. When several Italian girls in my class discovered that I didn't even know what pizza was, they felt it their patriotic duty to enlighten me. That required a visit to their favorite nearby pizza parlor, where I discovered that authentic New York pizza, which burned your mouth and threatened to drip gobs of liquid mozzarella on your lap, was *good*.

We kept a lookout through the window for any sign of a nun's black habit, and ducked when necessary until they passed. We had a feeling that they knew we were there but couldn't be sure.

It was at Saint Angela's that I recognized a new future possibility. I had never thought about whether I was smart or not, but it seemed everyone in school thought so, and my grades were the highest in the class. Since my family had no money for college but it was taken for granted that not going was not an option, the idea that I might get another scholarship for that purpose took root.

I had not known before getting the scholarship to Saint Angela's that such a thing was possible, but apparently America was a country where academic achievement paid off. Perhaps that could become the currency for my further education.

The nuns facilitated this by never letting me get away with doing less than my best. Because I found schoolwork easy, I was more inclined to do just enough to get the expected grades and focus on social life or reading books like *War and Peace, The Brothers Karamazov*, and various historical romances, all excluded from our reading list. But because of the scholarship dream, whenever an invitation to further expand my extracurricular activities was extended, I readily accepted. It was usually a command performance anyway.

I also came to realize that being a foreigner, while making me an outsider to the main social groups in the class, had a surprising aspect. It kept me from getting involved in ongoing rivalries or having to follow any particular group's norms, and therefore made me a neutral compromise candidate for the Student Council even though I would not have sought that role on my own.

It seemed that being different had a bright side even if outweighed by the pervasive loneliness of not "belonging."

My search for the meaning of life, born in the midst of our chaotic wartime odyssey, made me open to Catholic teachings, but I couldn't buy into the kinds of sins they said would send me to Hell.

Having already seen something like a real hell right here on earth, I couldn't believe that a loving God would eternally condemn anyone for not following rules made up by men, or what men thought God meant.

Personally, I didn't think men were smart enough to always know "God's will." I also believed that the Virgin Mary had to be divine. If Jesus was divine, it was obvious to me that his mother had to be also. As far as I was concerned, learning about her was the best part of religion class.

I loved the idea of a feminine divinity, but I never shared that with anyone.

What I did learn was a deep respect for the Sisters—for their kindness even when stern, their commitment to serve their God through teaching and caring for us, and their tireless efforts to nudge us toward excellence. Theirs was the task of Sisyphus, and we were their boulders. I began to see that they were not being picky or mean. They cared, not just about us but also about what they were teaching.

That I was required to learn Latin was a surprise.

"Why do I have to study a language no one speaks any more?" I moaned to my parents.

Father was pleased. "Someday you'll be glad to have that foundation," he said with a smile. Yeah, right, I thought.

I had to admit, though, that Sister Miriam taught with a passion that made it interesting and gave us a real feel for everyday life in the Roman Empire. She even looked Roman to me, and managed to make translating Caesar's conquest of Gaul almost bearable.

After the two required years, I balked at her decree that I was to continue into the third year, as well as continue the Latin translation contests she made me compete in on Saturdays, after I'd had too little sleep from having danced late into Friday night. My father was no help when I again complained, still saying I would someday thank Sister Miriam. He better be right, I fumed, especially since I had no choice.

Sister Naomi's gift to me was less academic. Although she never had cause to complain about my performance in algebra or geometry, I was not enthusiastic about math. I liked her class because she exuded a gentle goodness that brightened the room. I thought she was young, although shrouded in her habit, with only her pretty face visible, it was hard to tell.

She was more open-minded than some of the other teachers, and when "correct" textbook procedures in geometry did not work for me even though my answers were correct, she asked me to explain my quirky path to the answers and ended up giving me full credit. I admired her for this flexibility—and for her unfailing kindness and respect for her students.

Sister Dorothy Thérèse was my favorite. She taught me French and served as a friend I could go to with problems, or just to talk about France. She looked deceptively stern, with an imposing presence, but had a puckish sense of humor and a broad worldview. I felt few constraints with her on what was an "appropriate" topic. I often wondered what had led her to become a nun, but never had the nerve to ask. I had the feeling that she had suffered deeply in some way, but probing would have crossed the line.

She loved all things French, and generated in me a passionate desire to go to France—Paris in particular.

I learned the language with ease, as though "remembering" rather than learning, very different from when I'd been forced to learn German during the war. The ease with which I learned French defied logic—as did a strange experience I never shared with anyone.

With only two years of instruction under my belt, I started to dream complex poems in French, which I could neither understand nor reconstruct while awake. Yet I knew I had fully understood them in the dream and could recognize them if I actually saw them in writing. That strange experience further fueled my determination to go to France someday.

Two other nuns went out of their way to boost my skills for navigating college. It would be fair to say that they bullied me into excellence.

Sister Saint Agnes was relentless in her pursuit of perfect English. She made us diagram endless sentences, and woe unto anyone whose sentence structure or spelling was sloppy. She drafted me to write a column for the school paper, work on the yearbook, and had us memorize and present to the class a book report as a demonstration of elocution skills.

Even with only classmates as an audience, I was terrified and, having survived it, hoped I would never have to give another memorized speech in front of *any* audience.

Public speaking was part of the curriculum, however, taught by a visiting acting coach—a colorful, quirky little bird of a woman, with bright hats as plumage and modeling histrionic poetry recitations for us that we couldn't possibly emulate with a straight face.

When a citywide writing contest sponsored by the American Legion was announced, we were asked to write an essay. To my dismay, mine was chosen for presentation, this time to the whole school. Fear of stumbling and embarrassing myself on stage flooded me, but the sisters turned a deaf ear to my plea that someone else read it for me.

Somehow I got through it, but then things got worse: I had won what I didn't realize was a contest, and was chosen to represent the school at the citywide oratory tournament. That one was open to the public. The sisters congratulated me heartily and said they looked forward to my performance. All I could see ahead was disaster.

"Please, no! I can't do that," said I in panic.

"Yes you can, and you *shall!*" said the sisters.

There was no appeal. I spent the next several weeks rehearsing with them to the point where I could recite that speech in my sleep, but as the date approached, my panic ballooned. The day before, I came down with laryngitis and could barely croak.

The sisters didn't buy it. They made a bottled concoction of warm lemon water with honey, which I was to carry with me and sip frequently. Every teacher throughout the day reminded me: "Drink!" It was a conspiracy from which there was no escape.

The next day, my parents accompanied me to the contest hall, where I felt like I was moving in a dream. I had to keep my knees from buckling as I mounted the stairs to the podium, and the rest was a blur. The speech seemed to happen on its own.

When it ended, there was applause as I focused intently on making it back down the stairs without stumbling. It was utter relief to sit down and have the ordeal over with. A little later, starting to relax, I heard my name called again, followed by more applause. Once more, I managed to walk up and back down those stairs. I went home with a medal, my parents were thrilled, my school was proud, and I was stunned.

That was not the end of it either. Sister Maria Regina, our history teacher, decided I should join the debating team and participate in citywide tournaments. Then, as I became more comfortable with speaking in public and our team brought home some medals for the school, the sisters decided I should also participate in extemporaneous oratory tournaments.

These involved randomly drawing a topic from a basket, having about fifteen minutes to prepare, and then, with no notes, delivering a speech of similar length in front of judges. It actually got to be fun after I learned to cope well enough with stage fright to stand without wobbly knees. The growing comfort with public speaking on stage began to feel good.

In both English and American history, especially during the senior year, Sister Maria Regina made us repeatedly polish long, referenced research papers and, when I inquired why I had to do more revisions on a paper she had already said was good, the answer was always some version of, "You can make it better." She said it would prepare me for college.

In their relentless pursuit of perfection, the sisters drove me to a level of performance I would not have pursued on my own. As my father said about Latin, I would probably appreciate it later. Or so I hoped. As long as I also had room for my social life, I was happy to go with the program.

Chapter 21

DANCING BETWEEN CULTURES

All this time, my life felt like a dance between two cultures, not fully belonging to either. Two years into high school, I still had no citizenship. My parents had become US citizens as soon as their five years of residence were up, but I had to wait until I turned sixteen and became eligible to apply on my own.

It was a festive day when it finally happened, with my whole family and several friends joining the celebration. I finally had a legitimate home country. But that didn't really affect my everyday life.

School days were serious; Friday nights and weekends were for fun. Friday was the night Estonia's transplanted youth converged on Estonian House in midtown Manhattan to dance, to flirt, to find out who liked whom, to see who would get asked to dance by whom, and whether the person we hoped would show up actually would. The anticipation built through the school week to a crescendo on Friday afternoon.

I noticed that our dating game was less structured than the American custom of having a specific boy-friend or girlfriend—or not. For us, the lines were blurry. There were mixed groupings that tended to hang together, sometimes pairing up and sometimes not. Unless two people had indicated that they were a couple it was fine for them to date or dance with anyone they wished.

The boys were expected to do the asking, while the girls waited with fluttering hearts for "the one" to ask. If "the one" asked someone else, we pretended not to care and made a point of finding another part-ner. The identity of "the one" varied. It could be a temporary crush, a more lasting interest, or even a serious commitment that meant marriage.

The elements of possibility and uncertainty lent suspense to every weekend and every social event. After dancing a couple of hours, we would descend on the soda shop around the corner on Second Ave-nue for hamburgers and coke. It was there our group really got to know each other and made plans for fur-ther get-togethers. After the caloric reload we would either go home if it was late, or cruise around town.

Girls were always accompanied home—quite a trek for my escorts, particularly late at night on the subway. It was a long ride with a sparse schedule, and since we were scattered all over the different bor-oughs, whoever was willing to escort me home had to like me enough to then take an even longer ride back to his own home.

This was socially expected gentlemanly behavior, so I took chivalry as an explanation for boys' willingness to do this for me. I was always unsure how they really felt, and too insecure about my own appeal to assume anything that was not explicitly said. Since boys rarely expressed feelings, their shyness elicited mine in response.

I never discussed school with my Estonian friends, or my weekend activities with schoolmates.

My school grades were top secret as far as boys in our social circle were concerned. They saw me as a good dancer and fun to hang out with, while at school neither nuns nor classmates could have imagined me in the middle of a dance floor doing a jitterbug with petticoats flying. To them I was simply a smart student, liked but "different."

To me, these were two separate worlds, each for an aspect of "the real me," each comfortable in "her" own world. I kept it that way until Saint Angela's Senior Prom, where the two worlds collided.

My date was TK, as his college friends called him, a strikingly handsome junior at Princeton I had met earlier in Lakewood, New Jersey, during the summer I turned sixteen.

He and I didn't connect right away. I had heard some other girls talking about this gorgeous guy who lived in Lakewood, but he was three years older than I so we hung out with different groups.

What Estonian House was to the New York émigré community, the Lakewood Estonian Club was to its mid-Jersey counterpart, with sports, dances, and other social activities in high gear during the summer months. Located ten miles from the Jersey shore, with two lakes within the town itself, Lakewood had become a summer vacation spot for many New York Estonians, who added big city energy and a party mood to the local scene.

Our family rented one of the apartments in a multiplex for summer visitors called Ocean House. New York families we knew occupied the other apartments, making it a nice community.

Three grandmothers on site anchored the place and tended the children through the summer, while the working adults—including me during the summer before my senior year—hurried to the Port Authority bus terminal every Friday after work to get to "the country" as soon as possible.

From end of school to Labor Day weekend, our Friday and Saturday night social scene shifted from Manhattan to central New Jersey.

I had just arrived at the clubhouse one evening with several friends when one pointed excitedly toward a cluster of young people: "There's that guy I told you about. Doesn't he look like a movie star?"

He actually did. With outdoor lights illuminating the group, TK sat on a picnic table surrounded by a cluster of giggly girls. He worked summers as a carpenter for his father's construction firm, and his tall, well-muscled athletic body tanned beautifully. With his black hair, big blue-gray eyes, wearing a white shirt open in front to expose his chest, he was strikingly handsome. He obviously enjoyed the attention, openly flirting with the girls, and to me he looked like a conceited pretty boy, probably all brawn and no brain.

"Looks like he thinks he's God's gift to women," I retorted, and decided to ignore him.

One night soon after, when everyone was dancing on the outdoor basketball court, he asked me to dance. I had noticed that he was a good dancer, so why not, I thought. We discovered we had a natural chemistry on the dance floor, but since I had decided to ignore his physical appeal, I didn't encourage conversation and quickly rejoined my friends after the dance ended.

Yet in spite of myself, I couldn't help being aware of him after that.

Not long after, my parents and I went to see a movie. On our way out afterward, we ran into TK and a friend of his. In the course of discussing the movie, which we all liked, TK asked if I'd be interested in staying to see the last showing. Since we had not exited the theater, our tickets were still valid.

It would last until midnight, which concerned my parents, but TK assured them that he would see me safely home. Since he was part of the Estonian community, they figured he could be trusted, so TK and I stayed. I told myself I was staying for the movie.

We talked a lot as we walked slowly back to Ocean House, and I was surprised to find him genuinely interesting.

He had read most of the books I liked, and loved classic Greek drama. In fact, he turned out to be more intellectually stimulating than almost anyone else I knew. Without anything being said about "dating," we saw a lot of each other through the rest of that summer, and he was one of the conspirators who arranged a surprise "sweet sixteen" birthday party for me. I never suspected a thing.

His having gone to all that trouble felt very special. If his aim was to impress me and touch my heart, he couldn't have done any better. Aware that he was a flirt—some of the girls had nicknamed him Romeo—I didn't want to fall in love with him and get hurt, so I acted as casual as I could. But my heart had its own ideas.

It was a wonderful summer, even if he did disappear from my life after it ended. He returned to Princeton, where he also had a girl he was dating, and I returned to New York to complete high school and resume my city life.

I had almost let go of our summer romance when TK surprised me the following spring by calling and inviting me to be his date for Princeton's big weekend. I reciprocated the following spring by asking him to my senior prom.

We danced our hearts out, inspired by a great band and the gorgeous setting of the Plaza Hotel. We made no effort to tone down the tango, his dance specialty, even though it was a bit spicy for a religious school event. For me, this was an act of defiance.

At that point I didn't care what any of Saint Angela's officials thought. I felt betrayed. I was still in shock from an unexpected act on the part of the school that was contrary to their own tradition, an act that brought back all the painful feelings connected with the words "immigrant" and "different" just when I was feeling happy about my years as an integral part of the school.

It was traditional for the girl with the highest four-year average to receive the general excellence medal and be the valedictorian, and I knew that meant me. The salutatorian was by custom the next highest achiever. I had looked forward to the top honor, not so much because I wanted to write and memorize yet another speech, but because I knew how much it would mean to my parents.

A week before graduation, right before the prom, I realized that no one had talked to me about the speech. That was strange, because they always prepared for such events early. Then it was announced at assembly that the girl just below me in GPA would deliver the valedictory, and another would give the salutatory. I would, however, still get the general excellence medal.

I was shocked. So were my classmates. Being familiar at that point with Catholic parochialism, I could understand why they had preferred that the equally accomplished student they had chosen be the prime voice of the class in front of all the Catholic parents and friends, but why also exclude me from being salutatorian?

Like a blow to the gut, I got it: I was not considered a suitable public voice for the school, even after the honors I had earned. They were deliberately pushing me out of the limelight. What hurt even more was that no one had told me ahead of time.

I had noticed a subtle unease in my favorite nuns when interacting with me, but dismissed it as just imagination. I guessed there were some among them who did not agree with the decision, but no one said anything. Instead, they became more distant. I wondered whether the decision had come from a higher level of the hierarchy, but there was no way for me to find out. Perhaps they were not free to speak.

I finally approached Sister Dorothy Thérèse. She looked sad and empathized with my feelings. Though she did not say so explicitly, the message came through that she felt I had been treated badly and should at least have been warned privately before I had to hear the news at assembly. Her support was some comfort, but didn't make it easier.

I tried hard to hide my hurt and, at this point, anger. I felt my parents had been cheated even more than I, but they took it with their usual grace. Father pointed out that I had been given an excellent education at Saint Angela's—for free—and a bias for showing off one's "own" in preference to a foreigner during such an important celebration was simply human nature.

"I am so proud of your graduating at the top of your class," he said gently, "and how they choose to conduct their ceremony doesn't take away from what you've accomplished. Just keep your disappointment to yourself, hold your head high, and be your best self."

Mother agreed. But it was still not okay with me. Though determined to enjoy the prom anyway, I no longer felt I belonged there. Hence my defiant tango.

Yet another disappointment awaited at the commencement ceremony.

The school took pride in announcing all the graduates' college admissions and scholarships. We had been strongly encouraged to apply to Catholic colleges, so to please the nuns I had included one exclusive Catholic college on my list that I was sure would not accept me. The other three were Seven Sisters colleges, too secular to meet with the school's approval.

To my surprise, all of the colleges I applied to accepted me, and to the nuns' dismay, I chose Mount Holyoke, the oldest of the Seven Sisters schools. The official reaction became plain at graduation. While I had gotten the most acceptances and total scholarships, only two of mine were announced: the New York State scholarship, usable at any college in New York State, and the Catholic college. The three schools they disapproved of were omitted.

I then realized that perhaps my choice of a secular school was actually the main reason for my exclusion from being a speaker. I felt doubly betrayed.

I put on a good face through the ceremony and obligatory social exchanges afterward, and made a point of saying a sincerely warm thank you to those classmates and teachers who had been especially kind. The love and gratitude I had felt for the enormous gift they had given me vied internally with waves of indignation at what I saw as rank prejudice.

I told myself that soon my life in a much bigger world would begin, and in time none of this would matter, but it was hard to maintain my composure. The long childhood practice of braving on got me through.

Relieved when it was over, I walked away, and vowed to never go back.

Chapter 22

COLLEGE DREAMS

A year before I arrived in South Hadley, a pictur-
esque hamlet nestled in the mountains of western
Massachusetts, I had never heard of Mount Holyoke
College.

This first college for women in the United States,
founded in 1837 by an enterprising pre-feminist
named Mary Lyon in the face of patriarchal resistance and ridicule, was dubbed "college of the uncommon woman" by its President. That I ended up
there was pure serendipity.

During the last years at Saint Angela's, my college aspirations had been confined to the New York
area where, assuming I won a New York State scholarship, I would have had some funding, and com-
muting from home would have saved money.

That plan made sense, but in my heart I desperately yearned to go away to college and live on campus.

Ever since attending Princeton's big spring weekend as TK's date and falling in love with its campus, that kind of environment had become part of

my dream of a "full college experience." The idea of studying and living with intellectually engaged peers, on a beautiful campus with abundant trees and architectural beauty, was everything I could ever hope for.

It became my "impossible dream."

Although I was the only date at the Princeton weekend still in high school, I had felt quite at home with the older girls and asked them a lot of questions. Many were from Seven Sisters colleges. That was the first I knew of the men's "Ivies" and women's "Seven Sisters" colleges, and realized that a women's college would be perfect for me.

I would not be distracted during classes by trying to impress some guy, so I could focus on academics during the week yet have ample opportunities for dating on weekends. I would have to maintain high grades to keep the scholarship I would need to attend such a college, and this kind of bifurcated lifestyle had served me well through high school.

My friend Gerry planted the seed of actively reaching for my dream. She was a classmate who lived fairly close by, and we often rode the bus to school together.

I got to know her parents, who strongly encouraged me to aim for the top schools because they thought I was a good candidate for a scholarship. If not for that encouragement and many hours spent poring over the catalogs Gerry lent me, I probably would have stayed near home.

From its catalogue, I fell in love with Mount Holyoke. The photographs looked like my dream campus, the course selections were mind-boggling, and their having a Junior Year Abroad program with fully transferred credits sounded almost too good to be true. When I saw that Paris was one of the options, I couldn't contain my excitement.

Come what may, I was going to apply, and the application process would be simplified by my having become a U.S. citizen.

So I did, without official recommendations from Saint Angela Hall. They "could not" recommend my going to "such a school" — presumably full of non-Catholics and moral dangers — and only provided the minimum obligatory information in support of my application. Barnard and Wellesley were equally unacceptable to them.

With scant hope of success, I still persisted because I did not want to live with future regrets for not trying. What did I have to lose? After mailing the forms packet, and since the Holyoke catalog offered the possibility of a personal visit and interview, I decided to experience the college and campus first hand. At least I would have seen it even if I didn't get to attend.

I wrote and made an afternoon appointment with the Admissions Office and researched the train schedules from New York to the city of Holyoke. From there, a bus would transport me to the campus in South Hadley.

On the designated day, with nervous blessings and a promised excuse for that day's absence from school from my parents, I set off on an early train from Grand Central Station.

After five hours, having easily found the bus connection, I walked into the office of the Dean of Admissions, who turned out to be the one conducting my interview. She was a pleasant, attractive middle-aged woman who shook my hand warmly but looked surprised.

"Where are your parents?" she asked.

"In New York," I responded, equally surprised.

"You mean you came all this way alone? Your parents are not with you?"

"They both work, and I came by train. It was easy."

"And you took the bus from the station to South Hadley?" She made it sound like a major feat.

"Yes," I said, stating the obvious. I was here, wasn't I?

I was beginning to wonder why the way I got there was becoming an issue. What I did was logical. Neither parent could easily take off from work, they were not part of the interview, and the cost of two or three people traveling would have strained the family budget. Besides, a comfortable train ride was actually much safer than navigating the New York subway system, as I had been doing for years.

I had no idea that other applicants were usually accompanied by parents. Had I known, I would have understood her reaction to my solo appearance from so far away. But to me what I was doing made perfect sense.

The Dean looked at me quizzically, and we proceeded with the interview. It was clear that I had made an impression; I just couldn't guess what kind.

She praised my school record and College Board scores, which I didn't know because they were not released to students. I was glad to hear they were high. I told her of my love of languages, interest in studying French and hoping to study in Paris, and as much about my early background as she specifically asked. Our conversation flowed with surprising ease.

She then decided to personally take me on a tour of the campus—which totally exceeded my expectations. It was said to be one of the most beautiful in the country, and I could see why.

I couldn't contain my enthusiasm. Being able to go there would be my dream come true, but the fact that this nice person was going out of her way to show me around didn't mean I would be accepted.

And even if I were, I would need a lot of financial support to actually attend.

I think at some point her maternal instinct kicked in, because when it was time for me to leave she insisted on driving me back to the train and making sure I was safely on my way home. She also insisted on feeding me a hamburger at Glessie's—a drug store and soda shop right off campus where students hung out to eat, study, and refuel with caffeine.

All in all, I left with a good feeling about my visit, and I got to tell the Dean in person how very much I wanted to attend Mount Holyoke.

I returned to my everyday life in New York to anxiously await what the future would bring, or not. Acceptances would not be sent out for another month. I had my heart set on Holyoke now and felt deep down that I was meant to go there, but it would be an anxious time before I found out whether the college agreed.

When the acceptance letter came, I was ecstatic. It included the offer of a four-year Gould Foundation scholarship, awarded to one freshman student each year and renewable annually—assuming acceptable grades, and I would work hard to make sure of that. The letter ended with a handwritten postscript from the Dean saying how much it pleased her personally to offer me not only acceptance but also this special scholarship.

It was a kind gesture that made me feel truly welcome when the time finally came to leave home for my dream-come-true college adventure.

Driving through the antique iron gate that marked the official campus entrance for my first year as a member of the Class of 1960 felt momentous. And freeing. I knew I would take full advantage of the sumptuous intellectual banquet that awaited me, and perhaps now I would finally feel at home in America, as an American.

Although I was to live within the cocoon of the school, which functioned *in loco parentis* (as parental substitute) in maintaining adherence to rules, I still felt essentially on my own in this new environment. It was up to me to make a life here in the midst of so many bright, confident young women.

Not being a particularly organized or disciplined student, and given that I was about to step onto a much bigger stage than before, I resolved to shape up to keep up—whatever it took. The gift of education I had been given for a second time warranted no less.

In spite of the unfortunate ending, I felt the deepest gratitude to the nuns of Saint Angela Hall for preparing me, in spite of myself, for this new life. It was now up to me to be worthy of their efforts.

Chapter 23

INDELIBLE IMPRINTS

TK was not part of my life during freshman year or the following summer. He had drifted away after my prom. I plunged into college social life quickly to bury my disappointment.

There were lots of young men coming to campus, and invitations to visit their schools for various happenings—football weekends, fraternity parties, and special events.

Yet I couldn't forget TK. His image hovered in the back of my mind, which kept anyone else from getting a foothold on my affections. In spite of this, my imagined "full college experience" was in full swing.

Barb, my assigned first year roommate, was delightful, and a group of us in Porter Hall became friends. Betty, a lovely ethereal being with a backbone of steel, in love with art and poetry, became a special friend and then my roommate during sophomore year, when a group of us decided to move *en masse* to the French House instead of a regular dormitory.

A large white New England-style house on the edge of campus, more homelike than a dorm, it was intended for language immersion with French the only language spoken in common living areas. To make sure this happened, we had a native French housemother.

Francine was a graduate student from Versailles, just outside of Paris, and functioned more like an older sister than a "mother." She did not have the temperament to be an authority figure, which suited us fine. She considered some of our rules for essentially grown-up girls rather silly.

From time to time she took off to Boston for a weekend with friends, leaving us on our own. There was a tacit understanding that we would not mention her absence, nor behave in any way that would call attention to our dorm. She treated us as friends and equals, and we responded in kind by keeping our end of the bargain.

Marisol, another French graduate student from Paris, visited almost daily and became our second "big sister" as well as informal language coach. She and I hit it off especially well and became friends.

It was a lushly expansive year full of laughter and camaraderie, much to the credit of our professors, many of whom left indelible imprints on my character and worldview. With such a remarkable faculty, whom we addressed as Mr., Mrs., or Miss rather than academic titles, each of us developed special mentoring relationships, usually but not always in our areas of special interest.

Paul Saintonge, Chair of the French Department and my major advisor, left an indelible imprint. He was animated, worldly, and very French, with a love of theater and a penchant for performance. He exuberantly dramatized all literature, whether already in dramatic form or not, and insisted on drilling down obsessively into all the possible arcane meanings of everything we read.

Because of my affinity for the language and comfort with being on stage, he always cast me in the French plays he directed.

I loved it, as I came to love the whole process of staging a play: tryouts, casting, rehearsals, living into a character, performing, audience reaction, and the final performance when the curtain comes down for the last time on that particular production.

That was always a poignant moment, but I knew that nostalgia for the camaraderie and fun of being a member of that particular cast and crew would soon be replaced by the excitement of the next.

Falling in love with theatre led me to create a double major in French and Drama, a combination that had not been "on the books" before.

Aside from focusing on the two subjects I loved, this choice served the more practical purpose of alleviating my parents' concern that majoring in theatre alone would not provide me with a reliable livelihood after graduation. Mastering French would open the door to becoming a teacher or translator.

The gracious and witty Connie Saintonge, Paul's wife and my freshman English teacher, began our literary immersion by plunging us deeply into a dissection of the endless symbolic allusions within T.S. Eliot's *The Waste Land*, with all its intimidating complexity.

The task took the better part of the first semester, but provided amazingly diverse riches of cross-cultural information and fed my love of poetry. And her "you can make it better" responses to my own writing efforts had the familiar ring of high school.

The broad requirements of the liberal arts curriculum were a surprise, including basic courses in English literature, a foreign language, history, a physical science, a social science, a biological science, history of music, arts, and physical education, which even included passing a swimming test in order to graduate.

This last requirement almost did in one of my classmates who was incapable of floating without moving for sixty seconds. She had no body fat and sank straight to the bottom every time. After numerous futile attempts, the administration caved in and let her graduate.

Without this diverse mandate, I would never have studied astronomy, which instilled awe at the mystery of the universe and revived the interest my father had awakened in childhood.

An unexpected benefit for my personal health came from a course I would never have taken by choice: human physiology, including lab. Despite squeamishness about dissection and pricking my finger to determine blood type, I became fascinated by the intricate elegance of how the human body works and ended up wanting to learn more.

I was also eager to study psychology, thinking it might lead to a minor, but my interest in what makes humans tick did not extend to pigeons and rodents.

Understanding the power of conditioning did help, though, when I applied it to humans. So much for preconceived notions, though I still decided I was learning more about human nature from literature and theatre.

Amid this abundance, the deepest and most significant experience of the first two years was Mr. Leonard's course in European history, which met at 8:00 a.m. on Tuesday mornings, a class time I usually tried to avoid. Even at that hour, his classroom was packed.

He looked more like Abe Lincoln than any other man I'd seen, without a beard but tall and lanky with a simple but eloquent way of teaching. He was passionate about our turbulent human journey through the centuries from Greek times to the present, and how we create culture and belief systems to navigate the tides of history.

His love of the intricate layers of the human story was contagious. His assigned three-page "think pieces" throughout the year focused on existential questions inspired by classic writings from Plato and early Christian writers through Renaissance giants and modern political philosophers.

His style was very American—folksy and humorous—with a quick sense of humor and a genuine respect for students.

He taught us to think deeply and to adopt multiple perspectives, never tolerating glibness or empty rhetoric. For someone seeking authentic answers to questions about what it means to be human and live a good life, Mr. Leonard was a master catalyst.

His method was Socratic—not giving answers but showing us how to live into the questions and find our own. He was the teacher I hadn't known I was looking for who inspired me to wrestle with questions I had never thought to ask.

A familiar sight at Glessie's was a group of us sitting with him around a table, drinking endless cups of coffee while discussing anything and everything for hours at a stretch. He responded thoughtfully to even our more inane comments and, as long as we were interested and sincere, he was willing to give us as much time as we wanted. For that, he was soon to pay with his job.

He was not given tenure, reportedly because he spent too much time hanging out with students rather than producing research.

This made me aware for the first time of the "publish or perish" mandate for university faculty. Having learned this, I decided to exclude academia as a future career. I feared I would be too much like Mr. Leonard.

His loss was keenly felt by all of us who had benefited from his wisdom. I loved the richness of his responses to our papers, his comments overrunning the margins onto the back of the page. This ongoing dialogue meant more to me than an "A" at the end of the paper.

As my sophomore year progressed, thoughts of TK started to flit through my mind again, especially when out on a date with someone else. But with no contact for over a year, I had pretty much given up on him and decided to focus on going abroad for my junior year.

Then, out of the blue, an actual love letter arrived, asking if he could come to see me. I was surprised — and ambivalent.

Why now, when I was over him and so close to realizing my dream of going to Europe? To Paris yet. Some sensible part of me urged a firm No, but instead I wasted no time in saying yes.

TK and I resumed dating. Nothing had really changed from the times we were together before, except the pretense that the relationship was casual. Our union felt somehow inevitable. However, since I was determined to go to Paris, I was not prepared to make any commitments. I wanted to feel free in France to meet and go out with whomever I chose.

TK's history of ambiguous, on-again-off-again courtship felt too uncertain for me to limit other options. The timing of his sudden return also seemed suspect, as if he'd gotten wind of my plan to leave the country and wanted to "stake his claim" before one of "those Frenchmen" had a chance to "steal me away" — his own words when he owned up to his motives.

Perhaps he hoped his interest would change my mind about France. It didn't, even though whether I would be able to go was still uncertain.

The Sweet Briar Junior Year in France Program had accepted me, but I had applied without knowing where the money would come from and I had to respond soon. My scholarship was specifically for Holyoke, yet I had been so determined to go abroad that I figured it would be easier to apply and pull out if I had to than give up the dream before trying. Rational or not, I was hoping for a miracle.

As it happened, Mr. Meyer, CEO of the Gould Foundation, was about to arrive for his yearly visit to take all four of his scholarship recipients to lunch.

He was a friendly, thoughtful man who liked to hear personally of our interests and progress, and he happened to sit next to me that year. He asked how my French studies were going and I told him I had been awarded the first year French Prize, which seemed to please him.

I added that I was really hoping to perfect my French by spending the following year in Paris.

"Tell me more," he said.

He listened attentively as I told him I had been accepted by the Sweet Briar program, with all credits fully transferable back to Holyoke, but didn't think I could go. Then, without having even considered it a possibility, I heard myself blurt out:

"Would your foundation consider letting me use my scholarship in France? Assuming I maintain high grades, of course."

He paused for a few seconds, obviously surprised, and lapsed into silence. I couldn't interpret his serious expression, so I blushed, fearing I had been too presumptuous. His smile told me otherwise.

"I don't know," he replied. "No one has ever asked before. Your plan makes sense."

And, after another pause, "Let me talk to my Board. I'll let you know." In a daze of hopeful fantasy, I barely heard the rest of the conversation.

Within a week, I had the answer. They had researched the program and decided to grant my request. They would provide all the funds required, including tuition, room and board, as well as transatlantic transportation by ship. The sixty students in the program would sail as a group from New York to France on Cunard Line's *Mauretania*. Personal expenses would be up to me.

Amazing! Mr. Meyer's openness to changing rules when it made sense rather than sticking with "policy" had so easily fulfilled my "impossible dream." And because the American dollar was strong in Europe, the exchange rate would also save his foundation money: a win-win situation all around.

Except for TK, who was visibly disappointed about my leaving but tried to hide it.

When I boarded the ship for France in early September, he was at the sendoff with my family, including our extended family of old friends from DP camp who lived in the New York area and wanted to see the interior of a luxury liner.

TK's and my romance had blossomed during the summer before my departure, and we were very much in love. Saying goodbye to him was hard, but I had no regrets. Time would tell whether our relationship could survive a year's separation. He had been erratic in the past about writing letters, and for the next year that would be our only means of contact. I believed that his promise to "wait for me" was sincere when made, but would it endure?

Waving to them all as the ship pulled away, I was both skeptical and hopeful about TK and me, a little nervous about going so far from my family, and incredibly excited about what lay ahead.

My being on that ship felt magical. I hoped that returning to Europe, even if I could not go to my native land, would help me sort out who I was and where my life was meant to unfold. Was my "real self" European or American? Where might I fit in and create a fruitful life? Perhaps, when I came back for my senior year, I would have some answers. Even if not, the person I would be then would have learned a lot.

As I embarked on this unexpected dream-come-true adventure, I determined to open myself to the uncertainty of what this journey would bring, even if it took me out of my comfort zone.

Our group had already been herded together for a photograph, and there were a number of people who looked like they might be fun to know. Five leisurely days aboard ship would provide plenty of time to work on that.

The crew probably dreaded their yearly crossings with sixty rambunctious college kids aboard, but we were ready to ride the waves and have some fun. And we did.

Chapter 24

A New World

Having cleared customs in Le Havre, we were hustled into two chartered buses waiting to take us to Paris. With our mountains of luggage, we made quite a load, but everything found a place on board. We would stop overnight in Paris, then travel to Tours on the Loire River for six weeks of language immersion in preparation for the start of classes at the University of Paris in October.

Sixty pairs of eyes strained to take in the countryside and passing villages, eagerly escaping the bus when we stopped for lunch at Vernon, a small town in Normandy.

Our meal on the central square had been scheduled for a full hour, but some of us ate fast and took off to see the town, promising to get back in time. I wandered on my own to explore side streets where people actually lived rather than browsing shops on the main square.

From my first steps onto French soil, I had felt at home—a feeling of deep familiarity even though I had never even seen pictures of France before other than Paris. Turning a corner, I came upon my classmate Shirley, one of three Mount Holyoke students in the group.

I had only met her casually on campus, but we had become friendly on the boat and recognized each other as prospective buddies on this adventure. Looking starry-eyed, she walked up to me and, with her arms extended as if to embrace the whole town, exclaimed, "This is *mine!*"

"Same here," I echoed.

As we continued our walk together, we agreed to request each other as roommates when host family assignments were handed out. In most cases, there would be two of us to a family.

We met the director of the program upon our arrival in Paris, at a hotel off Boulevard Raspail on the Left Bank. We would continue to Tours the following morning. During that single night, several boys in our group managed to create a minor "international incident," resulting in a briefing the next day aboard the bus on the uses and abuses of *le bidet*.

Each room had one, more prominently placed than the toilet. Most of us had never seen one before and had no idea what its purpose was.

Shirl and I tried to guess, but gave up and decided that whatever it was, it was good for rinsing out stockings overnight. Unfortunately, several boys thought it must be a funny-looking foreign toilet, and used it as such.

That worked for liquids, but not for more solid matter. There was no flushing that down the little drain. Not knowing what to do, they left it there, in-furiating several disgusted maids. They complained to the hotel manager about these "American barbar-ians," which resulted in a call to our group leader.

Hence our diplomatically phrased briefing dur-ing the bus ride regarding proper bidet use.

Our language training at the *Institut de Touraine*, a study center for foreign students in the Loire valley, where the French language was reputed to be "pur-est," was to last six intense weeks. This would pre-pare us for plunging into the rigorous coursework we would face in Paris, which would require a com-mand of the language that few of us possessed on arrival.

We were assigned to local households to further enhance our French immersion. Shirl and I settled in with Mme. Proust, a sweet eighty-plus widow who turned out to be a marvelous cook and hostess, with a twinkle in her eye and an amused tolerance for our linguistic *faux pas* and other cultural gaffes. It was good that she did not speak English, because it forced us to use only French in her presence.

With grandmotherly tact and patience, she cor-rected us when necessary, and seemed to develop a genuine affection for us. The feeling was mutual. Our mealtimes rang with laughter, fueled in part by the ever-present and always good local wines.

I knew that remembering her would always warm my heart. She was a sterling example of how to age with humor and grace.

Our stay in Tours began with a party. The family of Claudine, another French student at Mount Holyoke during the previous year, lived in a vineyard her family owned. She had invited us to call when we arrived in Tours, and when we did she invited our Holyoke "gang of three" (Anne-Marie was the third) to a harvest party in their "caves."

There were some impressive cliffs on their property, with a network of connected, room-sized caves inside, some holding maturing barrels of wine and some configured for entertaining.

The reception was spectacular, with delicious food in one chamber, a wide selection of wines and other libations in another, and a dance floor with a live band in the largest one. All the spaces were illuminated with lanterns or candles.

The crowd was elegantly dressed, our hosts welcoming and gracious, and the band excellent. A rather attractive man started a conversation and soon, to my delight, asked me to dance. He danced well enough to be a pro, as he turned out to be.

He was on a break from touring with the internationally famous José Greco dance troupe, in Tours to visit his father for the weekend at their family estate nearby. He was Spanish, but his upbringing had been bi-lingual and bi-cultural.

We did well on the dance floor together. At one point we stopped and he spoke to the bandleader, resulting in a lively flamenco number next.

As he launched into a floor-stomping, hand-clapping rendition of this passionate dance form, he gestured for me to follow his lead. Although I knew the usual Latin dances like rumba, tango, and mambo, I'd had no previous experience with flamenco. The music was compelling, however, so I surrendered to the rhythm and mirrored his movements as best I could.

Then some kind of alchemy happened: an effortless flow of movement, totally in sync, no sense of me, or him, or time, or any other people in the room, lost in the dance itself—ecstatically free, with no thought or effort.

When the music stopped, it was like waking from a dream.

At first, I didn't grasp that the applause that I heard was for us, or that the room was packed with people who had apparently been watching us and clapping along.

I was too exhilarated to feel embarrassed, so we clowned with a theatrical bow. He was used to being on stage, and I'd had enough experience to follow his cues. Still, I was a little shaken by the experience. I hadn't known that dance, yet somehow I *became* it.

My partner decided that our being in sync on the dance floor warranted spending more time together. He would be leaving in two days, so I accepted an invitation to visit his home the next day and perhaps go riding before lunch. They had some nice horses, he said, thereby ensuring my consent. I loved horses.

Our leisurely meandering through the sunny autumn landscape on horseback the following day turned out to be yet another memorable experience. Afterward, his father—a florid flatterer whom I pegged as an incorrigible ladies' man—hosted us for lunch on the terrace. There was no sign of a "lady of the house."

Lunch was deliciously French and the conversation lively, but there was an aura of decadence and fading grandeur about the father and the house interior that I found unsettling.

The son was different, though, and dancing with him had been a transcendent joy I would never forget. As dusk approached, we said a warm goodbye and wished each other well.

On the serious side, the language instruction at the institute was demanding. Transportation for Shirl and me was walking or a rented bicycle, though some students bought Vespas and a few even a car, which enabled group excursions to the myriad tourist attractions of the region. Since Tours is the hub of some of the most famous *châteaux* in France, we could visit several even by bicycle.

My favorite vehicle was the Vespa belonging to Daniel, a charming Frenchman I met shortly after arrival. He, a friend of his, Shirley, and I did a lot of *château* hopping together, with Mme. Proust's approval. She knew the boys' families and pronounced them "respectable," even offering a cup of tea when they came to pick us up.

She took her role as chaperone quite seriously — but with a wicked wink.

If my heart had not been engaged with TK in spite of his not having written since saying goodbye in New York, my relationship with Daniel might have taken a more romantic turn than it did. The chemistry between us was undeniable.

As it was, however, we had wonderful times together talking, going to movies, and exploring castles. A tacit "just friends" agreement was mutually understood, given that I would be leaving for Paris all too soon. He went along with that, but there were moments of slippage.

When I left for Paris, our parting was ambiguous. Not quite goodbye, no promises either.

Our six weeks in Tours were up all too soon. We had to move on to the education we had come for, armed with intense drill in vocabulary, pronunciation, and writing papers in credible French. Though a struggle for some, all of us had made progress.

For a farewell celebration, to which all the students and faculty at the Institute were invited, we staged a scene from Molière's *Les femmes savantes* (The Learned Women). I both directed and reprised the role of Armande, which I had played during sophomore year at Holyoke. That allowed me to focus on the staging.

It took concerted effort for the cast and crew to pull it together so quickly, but the performance came out fairly well. Or so we were told—though the French tactfully omitted the qualification "for amateur foreigners."

Then, with tears and hugs, we left our cozy life with Madame, whom we would miss, and piled once again into crowded buses, this time heading north toward Paris. The closer we got, the more palpable our excitement.

I couldn't wait. My biggest dream had come true, by the grace of the Gould Foundation and its generous CEO.

Chapter 25

PARIS

A blonde little girl laughing, running
around and around a tree, tossing
golden leaves on the carpet that stretches
from the Arc de Triomphe to the Concorde.

Through the mist which even in sunshine
fills the air with the aura of Paris,
wheeled vehicles ricochet, honking
in the reddish glow of near-evening.

The sun sinks slowly toward setting,
bloody-eyed with the life that it carries,
lightly kisses the Tower of Eiffel,
leaving Paris to dream until morning.

Arm in arm, young lovers walk nowhere,
for Paris is theirs—they are Paris,
the little ones, they too belong here
and the growing, the aged, the dying,

the widow who smiles, though her wrinkles
have carved on her face a long story
of struggle, of love, and of mourning:
they all are the fabric of Paris.

And strangers—the blasé, the cynic,
the awe-stricken tourist, the timid,
they too, in their way, are of Paris
who welcomes them if they are willing
to love her—the life she is living
in beauty, in suffering, in giving.

I fell totally in love with Paris, and wrote this poem
on a glorious autumn day on a bench at the edge of
the Place de la Concorde. About a month had passed
since Shirley and I settled at the Foyer International,
a student dormitory on the Boulevard Saint-Michel,
right in the hub of the university district.

Our family placement had fallen through and this
was the only easily available alternative, although the
Sweet Briar administrator worried that we might not
have enough supervision. We promised to behave,
and we did in the ways that counted, but the freedom
from quasi-parental oversight was delightful. There
was no one to tell us where to go or what to do, or
worry if we stayed out late.

The Foyer did have some ironclad rules, so our
freedom had limits, but those were designed for security or frugality. The most bothersome were the
shower schedule and the curfew. We all occupied
small double rooms, with the bathrooms, toilets, and
a communal telephone down the hallway.

Showers with hot water were available for only two hours in the morning, so if you slept too long you were stuck with cold water or waiting till the next day—a choice Shirl and I exercised more often than we intended.

On weekdays, the front door closed exactly at midnight, and on weekends at one in the morning; if you missed it you were on your own until the door was unlocked again at seven.

A rule that bothered us was that two students of the same nationality could not room together. The idea was to get to know people from other nationalities.

I was assigned a French girl from Algeria, prissy and not particularly friendly, who got up early and ate her breakfast *biscottes* with sound effects reminiscent of a bunch of rabbits loose in a carrot patch. Her noisy eating always woke me up. Since I went out a lot at night and rarely got back before curfew, probably waking her in turn, it may have been retaliation.

Add a loud, talkative friend of hers who was there most of the day, and studying in my room became impossible. I spent most of my time in Shirley's room on a different floor. That worked because her official roommate was usually with her sister, also rooming with someone else.

This arrangement was inconvenient, but worth it for the benefits of living in the Latin Quarter within walking distance to our classes, not to mention the freedom it gave us. Most of the other students had to commute from farther-out residential areas.

The walk to the Louvre for our weekly art history class with M. Serullaz was the longest, but we got to stop at our favorite bakery on the way for chocolate croissants.

To say that we dove enthusiastically into the café-based social life along *"Boul-Miche"* (as our street was fondly known) would be an understatement. We aimed to have a genuine French experience across as broad a spectrum as possible, and to limit the time spent with other Americans.

Our standard hangout was Café Soufflot for socializing and Le Bac next door to the Foyer when we wanted to study in good lighting. The lamps in our rooms were monastically dim to save costs.

For the price of a coffee, we were free to sit there for hours, discussing and often debating every imaginable topic with whoever happened to come by, whether known or newly met. Formal introductions were not necessary among fellow students. Shirley and I never sat for long without someone asking to join us.

Our own building housed one of the government-subsidized student cafeterias. With an ID, you could eat for practically nothing at any of these and meet students from all over the world. They were popular places for socializing—in spite of the food, which belied the saying that one couldn't get a bad meal in France. On the bright side, the conviviality did foster international relations.

On Sundays, there were no classes and we were free to roam. Given very modest allowances from home, we settled for cheese and baguette in the dorm or outdoors at the Luxembourg Gardens unless we were invited somewhere for dinner or had a date.

The park was glorious on a nice day, and virtually across the street from Le Foyer, with a palace at one end, fountains where children sailed toy boats, walks and benches and statues, and lush lawn areas full of festive picnickers—a panorama of Parisian life to relish and absorb.

Once a month, the two of us were invited to a Sunday afternoon reception at the elegant home of a duchess in the 16th *arrondissement*, a high-end Paris neighborhood.

She invited a potpourri of Paris society from different walks of life, but we had no idea how we had landed on her list. We figured we probably filled a "nice foreign student" niche in the social mosaic.

Waiters in formal dress and white gloves paraded around with trays of luscious *hors d'oeuvres* and an endless supply of champagne. We met a lot of interesting people and, however we came to be there, the food was a welcome change from student fare. It was fun to dress up and have a delicious free meal by sampling all the offerings. We returned home happily sated and slightly tipsy.

My most enjoyable times were with Marisol and our former housemother Francine, both back home in France, who welcomed us to their world.

We met Francine's mother, a charming woman and wonderful hostess, who invited us to gourmet dinners at their apartment in Versailles and taught us about French life and gastronomy. It was in her home that Shirley met and fell seriously in love with Jean-Pierre, a friend of our hosts.

Marisol, whose family had several homes, spent a lot of time in Paris and we became ever better friends as the months rolled on.

Her family welcomed me warmly and, at a dinner I suspected was arranged for that purpose, she introduced me to two very different though equally fine men with whom I got to see and experience a range of Parisian life rarely accessible to visitors. I experienced Parisian "high society" from the inside with one, and artsy Montmartre with the other.

I felt more at home in Paris than anywhere I'd been since my early childhood in Tallinn. The idea of coming back after graduation to live and work there kept creeping into my mind, though I knew it would break my parents' hearts.

There was also TK, presumably awaiting my return. But he still hadn't written, and I didn't see any reason to limit my social life on his account.

It was glorious to be in Paris and free, meeting interesting male and female contemporaries, and especially older women who embodied the chic elegance that is seen as typically French but hard to describe. I had a lot to learn from them.

The profusion of male attention was a new experience. While I had never felt particularly attractive to American boys either in high school or in college, this was different, more like the flexible group-oriented socializing I had enjoyed with my Estonian friends in New York.

Shirl and I had many *copains* (buddies) rather than boyfriends, some in the Sweet Briar group and others with whom we cruised small cellar nightclubs scattered through the city—to dance, drink a little wine, and listen to popular singers.

Getting visibly drunk was considered *gauche,* so there was none of the drunken carousing I had seen at fraternity parties in the United States.

Seeing someone one-on-one did not automatically imply a romantic relationship or sexual intimacy unless it was "serious," implying marriage down the road. The French seemed to me less preoccupied with sex than Americans, yet talked about it more freely.

To be considered charming was a higher compliment than being "sexy." Someone who was attracted to you might at some point, over coffee, ask quite casually, "Would you like to go to bed with me?"

If you said no, the conversation would pick up where it left off—no problem. There was no pressure or manipulation, though verbal persuasion was not excluded.

The question might be repeated later, perhaps playfully: "Have you been overcome by my charm yet?"

If the answer remained no, the refused one might choose to still enjoy your company, or tactfully distance himself, in which case you would still be casually friendly when your paths crossed.

Though the implicit rules seemed simple, their individual applications were not. My friendship with J-P, one of the two men I met at Marisol's house and spent time with through much of the year, was complicated.

I was not romantically attracted to him in the way I was to TK or Daniel, but there was a mysterious mental and emotional bond that kept us going through cycles of ups and downs.

The downs usually had to do with my eclectic social life versus his wish to have our relationship be the priority. The ups were our thorough enjoyment of each other when we were in sync as just friends.

He was in some ways a mystery to me: complex, intelligent, basically still a boy—yet he easily disciplined me into being on time.

His method was simple. If I didn't appear by fifteen minutes past the designated time, he left, and there was no means of communication away from our residential phones. The issue was resolved, without discussion or recrimination, with my deciding that it was easier to make the effort to be on time. He always was.

When we weren't sparring over something, I found J-P deep, fun, and challenging, as well as sweet and comfortable to be with.

Although sampling the social life and mores of the Parisian elite was fascinating in giving me a feel for how the rich and titled live, I most enjoyed hanging out in Montmartre with J-P and his group of artsy-intellectual friends, especially a punster poet who liked to improvise on the spot.

We all collaborated on simple dinners that fit our student budgets. Often these meals consisted of a baguette and sardines with wine, and perhaps a piece of chocolate for dessert, but we had stimulating conversations and a lot of fun.

Around Thanksgiving, Shirl and I started exploring affordable ways to spend Christmas break. We discovered an unbelievably low-cost ski tour package for students to a village in Austria near Innsbruck.

The train ride took eighteen hours. With eight students in one compartment, sleep seemed impossible, but creativity saved the day.

We piled luggage in the space between the two facing benches to create a reasonably level area out of the whole compartment, and lay down across that space like a row of sardines. It was claustrophobic, but we did sleep a little, in spite of the snorer who apparently slept more than the rest of us.

Upon arrival at our inn, in the small village of Reith-Seefeld, we stashed our luggage in our rooms and rushed bleary-eyed to the slopes. I didn't know how to ski, but we had an instructor along, and I did learn to stay upright on the gentler slopes, even execute a passable snowplow.

I flunked parallel turns and stops, but got by with the "butt stop:" when you realize you are about to crash, sit down and rear-end traction will do the rest. There was a slight mishap, though, which I never lived down. I took down the instructor when my stopping maneuver didn't turn out as planned.

We landed in a contorted heap with skis askew. No one was hurt, but thenceforth he referred to me as *La Dangereuse* (dangerous woman).

I accepted my hopeless skier status with equanimity, and delighted in the dazzling beauty of the Alps under their sparkly pristine snow blanket, complemented by deep evergreen forests on their flanks, and dotted with gingerbread chalets both solitary and clustered in villages.

We celebrated Christmas at our inn with a cozy fire in an intricately carved fireplace, with good food and caroling in both English and German.

I felt a bittersweet pang when I noticed that the Christmas tree was decorated with the kind of real candles I had been used to as a child, but that long-ago memory was now more sweet than bitter and, so far from family at this special time, comforting.

The train ride back to Paris, much too soon, was a repeat sardine-can experience, but less claustrophobic and more fun. Sharing so many activities on and off the slopes for a week had bonded our group, which made all the difference.

The sleeping situation now generated hilarity, even though we didn't sleep any better. As we approached Paris, however, everyone seemed to become more subdued. Midyear exams were upon us in two weeks, so we all faced a cramming marathon as soon as we unpacked.

I don't think anyone had thought about exams during our Alpine playtime, but now it was clearly time to get serious—at least for a while.

Chapter 26

BOTHERSOME BORDERS

The travel bug had bitten in earnest. Exams were over and the grades good enough to assure the continuation of my scholarship, so it was time to turn toward planning our next adventure. Our trusty trio set about exploring viable options for the rest of the year.

We set Spain as our destination for Easter vacation, but transportation was a challenge. We also needed visas, which required navigating an arcane bureaucratic maze. Franco's Spain tended to be paranoid about people crossing its borders. Rather than being welcome, tourists were inherently suspect.

There wasn't even a direct train connection from Paris to Madrid, though had there been we would have ruled it out as too expensive. Yet Spain's being somewhat cut off from its more hospitable neighbors made it even more alluring.

We determined to make it work, but were engulfed in the meantime by classes and the rhythm of student life—the café culture again in full swing, but now indoors.

"I love Paris in the winter, when it drizzles," as the song says, was certainly true, but with a bone-chilling wind blowing through the numerous open spaces not directly sheltered by buildings, especially on the banks of the Seine, this love affair did have its questionable moments. Southern Spain's Mediterranean warmth sounded better and better.

Then, good news arrived. Shirl was dating an American soldier she had met in Austria whose friend was due for a leave during Easter week and had plans with another friend to go to Spain. When the prospective driver learned of our wish to do the same, he immediately offered all three of us a ride.

"What about our friend Marisol," we asked.

She planned to visit a cousin in Madrid, and thought it would be fun for us to go together. We would have to pick her up at her family's country house in Pau, in the Pyrenees close to the Spanish border.

No problem, his Chevy station wagon had plenty of room for all six of us, he said. We could all chip in for gas, and it would be fun.

What a stroke of luck! The skies of Paris suddenly looked less gray as we imagined ourselves in just a few weeks soaking up the sun on a beach. Then, bad news. Several days before departure, we got a phone call. The soldiers' leaves had been canceled, but they hoped to trade with someone else and still go.

We packed just in case, increasingly nervous as we waited for the final word. The dreaded call came the evening before they were to pick us up.

Now all our anticipation had been for naught and we would be stuck in Paris for the break, when in our minds we were already halfway to Spain. It was a dark day, and after trying to figure out how we might still go, we escaped into sleep early.

We had considered hitchhiking, but across two countries? With Spain having very few cars on the road and a dictatorial regime? Not a good idea.

The next morning Shirl and I dragged ourselves dolefully to Le Bac next door for coffee and buttered baguette, feeling depleted and defeated. After staring at our coffee for a while, we suddenly looked at each other, and one articulated what the other was thinking:

"Let's go to Spain anyway."

"Yes," was the immediate response, "you mean hitchhike."

"Of course. What's the worst that can happen?"

"We won't get enough rides, or get stopped at the border, and end up somewhere in France that we haven't seen yet."

"And if we get to Pau, we can stay with Marisol overnight and then hitchhike back."

"We'll have to repack. We'll be walking, so we can't take our suitcases."

"Okay, let's finish our coffee and get going. I told Marisol we'd be in Pau to pick her up by tomorrow evening."

"We can do it."

Then remembering, "We've got to call Annie to see if she wants to come."

Annie was the most practical of our trio, so we fully expected her to say we were nuts and she wasn't coming.

The first part of our assumption was correct. She said we were totally insane. Then she said yes.

We suddenly had a surge of energy. Wilting just minutes ago, we revived and our excitement grew by the moment.

Several friends, including J-P, came by to wish us a good trip, asking what time we'd be picked up. When we cheerfully informed them that our ride fell through, they looked bewildered.

"So how come you look so cheerful? You were really looking forward to this," one asked.

"We're still going, right after we finish our coffee," I said.

"Really? How?"

"We're going to hitchhike."

"You're kidding. You can't hitchhike all the way through Spain and back!"

"Well, we'll go as far as we can. If we don't make it, we'll be back in a few days. If not, we'll see you when classes start."

Our friends looked at us as if dealing with two lunatics. J-P put it succinctly:

"You've both lost your minds!"

We just nodded and laughed. They gave up and ordered coffee.

J-P inquired, with a note of sarcasm: "And I suppose you have an itinerary of some kind?"

"All we know is that we have to be in Pau by tomorrow evening. We're supposed to pick up Marisol."

I was rather enjoying his confusion.

"Does she know how you plan to get there? Or that you have no further transportation?"

"No, we have no way to contact her in time. So we'll tell her when we arrive," I smiled sweetly.

J-P rolled his eyes and sipped his coffee, mumbling only, "I wish you luck."

When we stood up to go and in turn wished them all a happy Easter vacation, his friend replied, "Well, we'll see you back here tomorrow."

We smiled smugly and hurried off, fully enjoying the brouhaha we had caused.

Now we were in a hurry. We quickly emptied our suitcases and cut our wardrobes down to a bare minimum of two pairs of washable slacks, several tops, a sweater, and a cotton dress, all rolled into a big tote bag.

We wore the only pair of shoes we would take, a raincoat over one of the slacks and top, and a handbag containing a wallet, camera, and needed toiletries. On the way, we stopped to buy maps of France and Spain.

We took several buses, ending up at the Porte d'Orléans at the end of the line, and walked to the highway toward Tours. Once there, we would improvise further, and if we got stuck, our dear Mme. Proust would surely help us. Having never hitchhiked before, we weren't sure how long it might take to get a ride.

Feeling terribly awkward, we gathered our nerve and hesitantly held out our thumbs. To our surprise, the first big truck to come along stopped and the driver said he could take us to Tours. There was room for all of us to squeeze into the cab with the friendly middle-aged trucker, curious to know who we were and what on earth we were doing hitchhiking on a major highway.

Our story seemed to amuse him, and when we got to Tours, he was careful to drop us off where we'd have the best chance to find the next ride.

And so it went. We got rides easily, found a hotel in a small town along the way to Bordeaux where we were dropped off at dusk, then continued the next day, arriving in Pau around five-thirty in the afternoon.

Our driver, another trucker, asked if we planned to continue further that evening. We said no, we had friends living nearby who would come and pick us up. Could he please drop us off somewhere with a telephone we could use? He looked dubious, but drove to a café he knew and made sure we could use the phone.

He stayed around for a drink, which we saw as a protective gesture toward these crazy girls. He had already pointed out to us, in no uncertain terms, the folly of trying to hitchhike through Spain.

I went to the phone and called the number Marisol had given me. She picked up quickly, delighted to finally hear from us, and offered directions to their house.

"We are not in a car," I said gingerly. "Our ride fell through so we hitchhiked. We're at Café Granville. Do you know it?"

There was dead silence at the other end for a moment, then: "You hitchhiked all the way here from Paris?! When did you start?"

"When we originally planned to leave. Yesterday around noon."

"That's amazing. Stay where you are. We'll send someone to pick you up."

The trucker was watching and listening with curiosity.

"Everything is fine," I told him. "Our friends are coming to get us."

He looked somewhat relieved and leaned back to savor his espresso. Then he wished us luck, repeated his opinion of our crazy scheme and, deflecting our expressions of gratitude with a shrug and "*de rien, Mesdemoiselles*," departed.

The man behind the bar asked us where we were traveling from there, and were we really planning to hitchhike through Spain? We said we would have to check out the train and bus situation, but we planned to cover Madrid, and then a loop of Granada, Malaga, Seville, Cordoba, and back again through Madrid to France.

He shook his head, "Well, I have to admire your guts."

By this time there were only two or three other people besides us scattered throughout the café. We had chosen an easily visible table as we waited for Marisol or her brother to come through the door.

When it finally opened, a uniformed chauffeur appeared instead, looked right past us, and announced: "Villa Navarre?"

I waved discreetly and nodded my head. His eyebrows shot up in astonishment, even more when he asked for our luggage and we pointed to our skimpy bags, but quickly recovered his formal demeanor. Obviously, we were not what he'd expected.

I could almost hear him wondering how Madame would react to these overgrown urchins. After two days mostly in trucks and nowhere to fully clean up, we didn't exactly look our best.

As we left, the wide-eyed bartender wished us luck and a safe journey. It would have been fun to see the trucker's expression had he still been there.

We drove out of the city in a large, comfortable car into what looked like spectacular countryside, though it was getting too dark to see much.

The appearance of the chauffeur had totally surprised me. I knew the family owned an apartment building in the best section of Paris, with various members having their own separate quarters. It was obvious they were wealthy, but I had never thought about it.

They were all warmhearted, down-to-earth people, we liked each other, and I felt at home with all the family members I had met. I never sensed elitism in any of them, least of all Marisol, one of the most authentic, brilliant, genuinely kind and uproariously funny people I had ever known. The "country house" had been mentioned in the course of conversations, but I didn't expect a mansion.

As we drove up a large circular driveway and stopped under the portico, Marisol and her mother, an American southerner by birth who had married and lived her adult life in France, were waiting for us.

The chauffeur relaxed visibly when Madame enthusiastically clasped me to her ample bosom, followed by Marisol greeting all three of us with a quip about our mode of travel.

We were quickly settled into a luxurious bedroom, and told to relax and change if we wished.
They would meet us in the dining room in an hour.
It had never occurred to me that the "country house"
they so casually referred to was their family's ancestral estate.

A warm shower and clean clothes did wonders.
We got lost on the way to the dining room even
though we'd been given directions, but managed to
join the family without need of rescue. They turned
the dinner into a celebration of our gumption in
sticking to our travel plan, however unorthodox the
execution.

Yet we did have to get practical about how to pro-
ceed, they said. Marisol, who we thought might bow
out of hitchhiking, said she wouldn't miss it for anything. Besides, there was safety in numbers.

After recounting our experiences on the road, and
our luck in getting rides from good people who got
us there on time, the talk turned to the serious challenge of how to get to Madrid, where we would have
a break for further planning at their cousin's apartment. Marisol was already expected to arrive there
with us, though by more conventional means, and
now we would need her cousin's help in figuring out
the transportation onward to Granada.

They all bemoaned the irony of having three cars
on site, with one readily available to Marisol, yet our
having to resort to hitchhiking because getting permission to take a French car over the border to Spain
was a bureaucratic nightmare we didn't have time
for.

It was decided that we would be driven to the border crossing the next morning and then catch what rides we could once across. Marisol would have to downsize her luggage, a challenge she readily embraced.

Dropping into our comfortable beds near midnight, we slept like babies. We knew the next day would be long and unpredictable. Luckily, we now had someone with us who spoke Spanish and had been to Spain before. That would be a real boon.

Chapter 27

SPANISH ESCAPADE

The next morning, after a hearty breakfast, we headed west toward Biarritz and then south on a two-lane road leading to a small border crossing, marked by a creek and a bridge. On each side was a small building manned by two border guards to check documents.

We stopped on the French side, the chauffeur opened the trunk and handed each of us our bags with ceremonial formality and a twinkle in his eye, then wished us *bon voyage* and drove away.

The French guards stared without moving, eyes wide and mouths open. Seeming at a loss for words, they stamped our passports and visas, looking across the bridge as though expecting something to appear on the other side.

We thanked them, walked across the bridge and repeated the ritual with the Spanish guards, who looked not only perplexed but also suspicious. Four girls, three of them American, arriving at the border with a chauffeur, then crossing the border on foot with just a few small bags and no visible means of transportation, was unusual to say the least.

Looking somewhat embarrassed, they searched our bags very thoroughly, then waved us on.

We held in the percolating laughter explosion until far enough down the road to be out of sight. Marisol said she'd heard a barely audible comment by one of the guards questioning our sanity in rather colorful terms. Who could blame them?

There was almost no traffic on the Spanish side, and four of us were too many for the average passenger car, so we decided to split into pairs if necessary and reunite in Madrid at Marisol's cousin's address.

After an hour or so, the first driver to stop said he could only take two as far as Burgos, so Marisol and I took off.

In Burgos, waiting for our next ride, we spotted Shirl and Annie at a nearby gas station on the main road. They were riding with a Cuban headed all the way to Madrid who was filling up his Mercedes. He agreed to take us, too. That took care of the first leg of our itinerary.

Cousin Charles, a tall, sandy-haired, handsome Texan living in Spain, was very helpful and offered to call some people to see if anyone they knew was planning to drive to Granada.

We retired early, exhausted from the day, but felt fine by morning. While Charles was preparing to call some friends, we headed to the Prado museum, the one place in Madrid we did not want to miss if a ride opened up that day or next. Rooms full of paintings by El Greco, Goya, Velasquez, and Murillo—the

Spanish fabulous four—were the magnet drawing us there. They did not disappoint.

Our enjoyment was soon interrupted by Charles, who rushed in and told us someone he knew named Pépé planned to drive to Granada in about half an hour, but would wait a little longer if we wanted to join him. Of course we did.

After a quick sprint through our favorite artists, we rushed back with Charles to pick up our things, piled into Pépé's car (sardine style—small car) and embarked on what I can only euphemistically call a "thrill ride," often at 120 km/hr. through narrow mountain roads with (literally) hairpin turns and precipitous drops that left no margin for error. With relatively few cars in most of Spain, and hardly any that we saw during our ride, there was nothing to slow him down.

It was terrifying. Still, as Moorish-style villages flashed by at warp speed, I also saw one of the most beautiful sunsets of my life, a vista from the mountains down to the glistening Mediterranean in the far distance—perhaps all the more beautiful because I feared it might be my last

Finally in Granada, still in one piece, we found a hotel. Our driver, cheerful and relaxed, took us all out to dinner and then offered to take us to some caves outside the city where gypsies lived and entertained tourists.

It was somewhat amateurish, he said, and you had to watch your purse, but the village, music, and dancing were authentic and worth seeing. He explained that in Spain young ladies did not go out in the evening without a male escort, and since he would be continuing farther south the following morning, this would be our only chance to be out at night.

It was an offer we couldn't refuse. We ended up tired but so glad we accepted. The performers looked somewhat scruffy, but they were accomplished musicians, especially one young man with a big gold front tooth who made a point of looking soulfully in our direction, as if singing only for us.

At one point, Marisol jokingly murmured, "Wow, he's just my type."

The dancers were also impressive. Even though we stayed for less than two hours, a short time by Spanish standards for an evening out, we were grateful to Pépé for a memorable evening. At our hotel, we wished him god-speed with heartfelt thanks, then collapsed into bed.

When Marisol and I went down to the lobby in the morning to meet the other two, the man at the desk handed us a note.

That was strange. We knew nobody in Granada, so we assumed it had to be from Pépé, but when Marisol opened it, she read: "The singer you admired last night will meet you at your hotel at noon." What??

The only explanation we could think of was that a waiter had overheard Marisol's flippant remark and taken it seriously. What would we do when he showed up? What was he expecting? Regretting the misguided levity that had obviously been misconstrued, we took the easy way out and left.

In spite of feeling like cowards escaping from an awkward situation, we thoroughly enjoyed our day at the Alhambra, and didn't return to the hotel until evening. We were too embarrassed to ask the desk clerk whether the man had shown up or not.

The Alhambra was, for me, the most beautiful site so far—with its lush gardens, clear pools, and Moorish architecture that nourished all the senses, enhanced by the background of a spectacular view of the city.

What appealed to me in particular was its soft, inviting human scale. Rather than seeing it merely as a historic monument, I could imagine living there.

As we strolled, we were surprised to encounter an American film crew shooting *It Started with a Kiss*, starring Glenn Ford and Debbie Reynolds, both of whom were active in the scene at hand.

Debbie, in the midst of the drama of her husband Eddie Fisher having left her for Elizabeth Taylor (the Hollywood scandal-du-jour), secluded herself in her trailer between takes so we only saw her briefly, but Glenn Ford hung out with the crew and invited us to join them.

He came across as a personable, genuinely nice man with no affected "star" aura. When I asked to take his picture, he readily agreed, and when I had trouble with my camera settings, he came over, set them properly, then walked back and smiled for the now functional camera.

I was charmed, and surprised at how natural our conversation felt. Still, it was thrilling to spend time with a famous movie star.

The rest of the day went quickly. We explored alleys leading to lush private courtyards and admired architecture straight out of *The Arabian Nights*—except that no one wore veils or turbans. The people were friendly and helpful, some of the men overly so, but that was not surprising considering how sheltered their own young women were. To see four of us traveling by ourselves around a foreign country was unusual enough to draw attention wherever we went.

It was not pleasant to always walk with an entourage of men trying to start a conversation or invite us to a café. Fortunately we never felt in any danger, nor were we ever physically accosted, so we learned to simply ignore them and pretend we were alone. Asking them to leave was only seen as encouragement. They seemed to think we should find their attention flattering. That it prevented us from fully enjoying their beautiful country was a message we could never get across.

Time was passing all too quickly, and the next morning we regretfully left Granada. The opportunity arose to crowd into a taxi to Malaga with two other tourists, and we grabbed it as preferable to hitchhiking or trying to figure out train schedules.

Given the dearth of cars and the cultural norms regarding what was proper for young ladies, especially in southern Spain, we felt it better to travel by conventional means when possible.

Though the car was very hot, with too many bodies in a small space, we had no complaints about the scenery. We arrived in Malaga in time to find a hotel for the night, eat, and look around a bit the following day before going on to Torremolinos, a beach resort nearby that we had been looking forward to since leaving Paris.

Finally, we were about to fulfill our idyllic image of basking in the sun with the Mediterranean lapping at our feet. Off-season, the town was quiet and relaxed, so there would be no crowds. Since it was late afternoon when we arrived, we hastened to find a place to stay, deferring the beach till the following day.

We found a small Swedish rooming house—Torremolinos was popular with northern Europeans during the winter—and an affordable German restaurant nearby. A leisurely picnic on the beach was our only firm plan for our stay. That night I wrote in my journal what I saw from our window to imprint the image in my memory:

> "Torremolinos is an unbelievably pretty resort town upon which the full moon is shining with heartbreaking intensity, creating a multitude of dancing patterns of flickering light on the Mediterranean."

The weather looked promising the next morning, but, by the time we had everyone organized for our lunch in the sun, clouds were rolling in. Undaunted, we went to the beach and had our picnic anyway, bundled up and freezing. We had brought no really warm clothing for the sunny Mediterranean of our fantasy. Adding insult to injury, it started to rain, so we threw in the towel and decided to go to Seville, hoping the weather would be better inland.

After a bus back to Malaga and a train to Seville, we arrived very close to eleven at night, desperate for food and a place to sleep. That was one time we were happy about the night-owl lifestyle of the Spaniards, because we did find an open restaurant and were directed to a cheap hotel nearby.

It was in a cold, musty, historic building with a minimum of basic amenities, but it would do the three of us for one night. Marisol had left us at the train station to stay with family friends who lived outside Seville, leaving us their phone number.

It was now Wednesday of Holy Week, a time of great devotion and public spectacles for the local people. The next morning, the sun came out and lifted our spirits.

We found a nice hotel right near the area where the main festivities would unfold. The grand parade, with magnificent statues carried prayerfully on a platform balanced on the shoulders of men from different parishes, each visibly proud of its decorated Virgin statue, was deeply moving and went on through the night. Our room had two small balconies that provided a bird's-eye view of the proceedings, but it turned out that I ended up seeing the parade very close up, from the VIP bleachers, until four the next morning.

The day of the parade, Marisol had called and asked me to come to a dinner party with her hosts, apologizing for not being able to invite us all. The weather was cool and all I had to wear was a simple cotton dress (thank goodness the hotel had an iron available) and a raincoat, but she assured me that what I wore was unimportant. Her friends just wanted to meet me.

When I gave the taxi driver the address, he said, "Oh, yes, the Marqués."

In packing for this trip, I could never have imagined that I'd be having dinner with the aristocracy of Seville, but there I was in my plain cotton dress, not having brought stockings and thus bare-legged, among an elegant group of fashionable, well-coiffed women (all wearing stockings, of course). Even Marisol was less casual than usual, having borrowed dressier clothes from her hostess. I felt like an ugly duckling amid swans, but Marisol's reassuring presence helped.

Our hosts were charming and welcomed me warmly. The ambiance was friendly, humorous, and informal. Everyone spoke French and English. My discomfort dissipated quickly as the multi-course feast ran its leisurely course.

When I thought it was time to leave, I didn't realize that the whole group would now go out to watch the procession from the bleachers on the big square, and that they took my participation for granted. Our host took me under his wing and explained each magnificent float as it went by, including the various symbolic meanings of what we were seeing.

He had seen this parade every year of his life, I guessed, yet he was as excited as a little boy, sometimes poking me in the ribs and pointing: "Look, look!" Although my ribs protested, his enthusiasm was endearing.

It surprised me to see these worldly, sophisticated people so emotionally moved by their city's age-old traditions. I really liked them, as I had everyone I had met through Marisol, regardless of where they fell on the social pyramid. Hers was an extraordinary family, and their friends seemed to reflect the old adage, "like attracts like."

As the hours passed, I became increasingly more exhausted, longing to sleep but not wanting to seem unappreciative when they were all having such a good time and being so kind. Finally, close to four in the morning, they decided to take a break for breakfast, and I took the opportunity to thank everyone for the extraordinary pleasure of participating in their celebration and to apologize for not being able to keep my eyes open any longer.

I really wished I'd had more stamina and not had to cut that momentous night short—if you can call four in the morning short. Despite my protests, Marisol and one of the men insisted on walking me to my hotel.

Shirl and Annie were fast asleep when I got to the room. I collapsed into bed and slept through their getting up and going out. I was still fast asleep when the phone rang around noon. It was Marisol. She had come down with a fever and was feeling quite ill. The doctor who had come to see her ordered her to stay in bed: no more traveling until she was fully recovered.

The news was a shock, since she had been so lively just a few hours earlier, but I was glad that it happened while she was staying with close friends who could give her the best possible care. What if it had happened on the road hitchhiking?

We stayed and explored Seville through Easter Sunday, even going to a bullfight, horrible yet weirdly fascinating in spite of my distaste for the cruelty involved. Luckily, this was not a game in which the bull was actually killed.

On Sunday afternoon, we went to say goodbye to Marisol. It was sad to lose her as a traveling companion. I hoped she would give herself the rest she needed to heal and allow her friends to take proper care of her, but knowing how hard it was to keep her down, I doubted it.

The next morning, we embarked on a five-hour train ride to Cordoba that turned out to be a nightmare: noisy, hot, and crowded with people staring at us. We decided that on our way back to Madrid, we would hitchhike instead.

We arrived in the late afternoon and spent the remainder of the day dealing with the basics of food and lodging, so the following day remained the only time we would have to see Cordoba. That day was magical, like the city itself: a fascinating Moorish-Spanish amalgam of culture and architecture. The high point for me was the huge, ornate mosque with a smaller Christian church built inside it—a unique monument to the city's multicultural history.

We experienced the people in Cordoba as warmer and friendlier than in the other cities we had visited, and that made our day there even more memorable.

The next morning, we had to continue back to Madrid and then northward to Paris. The final weeks of school, culminating in exams, awaited us, and we were cutting it close time-wise. We were lucky. The first car we tried picked us up and took us straight to Madrid—the driver a pleasant young fellow who only knew two words in English: "keess mee."

This time we spent three days in Madrid, completing our exploration of the Prado and catching more of the tourist sites, especially the huge, cold, and impressive Escorial, with a cathedral in the center and fabulous El Greco paintings. Then a side trip to Toledo, the forbiddingly grand capital of King Ferdinand and Queen Isabella's empire, with its overpowering Gothic cathedral.

We were lucky to be picked up on the way by a friendly Portuguese couple who invited us to tour with them, and so we saw more of Toledo than we would have on foot.

When we finally headed homeward, the first ride deposited us in Burgos, where we spent the night and our last Spanish money on two cans of sardines and a bag of breadsticks. We had to save enough of our French francs to get us home.

Early the following morning, we got a ride to a village in the craggy, desolate countryside of northern Spain, but no farther. Nobody was going all the way to San Sebastian, the closest city to the border crossing, much less to the crossing itself.

We sank into gloom as we sat roadside for almost two hours with not a car in sight. Finally we spotted a red Mercedes sedan speeding toward us. We jumped up and waved frantically.

It zoomed by, then stopped down the road and reversed to where we were still waving. A distinguished-looking white-haired man with a fatherly mien got out and asked what on earth we were doing there. When we told him, he shook his head in disbelief, as one might with misguided children.

"I'm going to San Sebastian, so you can come along," he said, "I would worry about you if I left you here. What would your parents think if they knew what you're doing?" We tried to look contrite.

It was the most luxurious ride of our whole trip, during which we told him the details of where we had been and how we had gotten there. He was amazed, and amused in spite of himself. He turned out to be the Belgian ambassador to Spain, on his way to San Sebastian because it was Generalissimo Franco's summer headquarters.

When we got there, he drove us around to see a bit of the city, a beautiful resort on the Atlantic coast with a long stretch of beach along the wide bay, and then took us to a café overlooking this magnificent view. He ordered drinks for all of us and asked if we were hungry.

We politely told him we were fine (with only the remains of the bread sticks and sardines for breakfast, we were actually starving). He said that he was hungry himself, and ordered what turned out to be a huge platter of tapas. Saying he didn't like to eat alone, he asked us to please join him—a gracious, generous act, and not the last.

He then insisted on driving us to the border to make sure we got safely back into France. He would have taken us to Biarritz, the first big city across the border, but of course he couldn't take his car across.

We were already acquainted with that problem. So we arrived at the Spanish side of the same bridge crossing as before, this time in a big Mercedes with shiny diplomatic plates.

The same guards as before stared in bug-eyed wonder as this distinguished gentleman handed us our bundles from the trunk, wished us a good trip home, and left. As before, we went through the document ritual, crossed the bridge, and once more walked down the road to wait for cars, heading north this time.

The guards' expressions were priceless, but we acted nonchalant, as though what we were doing were perfectly ordinary. Out of their sight, we chuckled about what stories they might concoct for their friends about their encounters with us.

The rest of the trip to Paris, driving with an assortment of fascinating characters, went quite easily, with an overnight stop at a small village. We arrived in Paris in time to go to a 4:30 class, but decided to skip it. Everyone would ask where we had been, and we simply didn't have the energy to answer yet.

After a good night's sleep, a shower, and some fresh clothes, however, we would be more than delighted to tell our story, with particular relish to those skeptics who had warned us that what we had just done was not possible. We resolved not to gloat too blatantly, but it would be difficult.

The magic of how smoothly our trip worked out was hard even for us to believe. For me, it had been an exhilarating taste of freedom and flow. With no extrinsic rules or expectations to follow, we could be as unfettered as our own intelligence and common sense dictated.

For someone who had always been a "good girl" and risen appropriately to any required occasion, such a feeling of total freedom was new. There was no one I had to account to for my behavior. I hadn't realized I had always felt I did, not because my parents demanded it—in fact they gave me a substantial amount of leeway and privacy—but because I had somehow internalized that imperative on my own.

Perhaps I had taken it on precisely because they trusted me so completely and I wanted to be worthy of that trust. I was beginning to feel an inner shift that I was not yet able to put into words. But it felt good.

Chapter 28

LAST LAP

Two days after we got back to Paris, we had tea with the Saintonges, who were visiting Holyoke's scattered fledglings abroad. Their ostensible reason was to check on how our studies were going, but we knew Monsieur would have taken advantage of any excuse to come to France.

Our academic report was easy. We were doing fine. Our Easter vacation story, however, made quite an impression. Laughing, they acknowledged that our experience had been "multifaceted" indeed, but they were glad to hear about it now that it was safely over.

No Sweet Briar official knew where we had gone, and because Shirl and I were not living with a family, there had been no one to worry about us, nor anyone to tell them. Now that we were experienced hitchhikers, we already had new plans for weekend outings closer to home.

Before anything new materialized, I received an unexpected visit from Daniel, with whom we had exchanged a few postcards but nothing more since my departure from Tours. He had received his draft notice and was going to be shipped to the island of Martinique.

That was a surprise to me. I hadn't known about his impending military service. It also surprised me that I was more excited to see him than I had expected, and sad about his leaving. Though we had not been in sync about the nature of our friendship, when I saw him again I realized that the attraction on my end was stronger than I'd wanted to admit. TK was still embedded in my psyche, so in all fairness I hadn't wanted to encourage Daniel, but my vacillation had fueled an ambivalent emotional attachment that was hard to break even though it had no realistic future.

Neither of us wanted to say goodbye, even though he was going far away and I would go back to America at the end of the year. The handwriting was on the wall, we both knew it, yet we decided to stay in touch by mail. Besides, TK had not written since Christmas, so I wasn't going to be foolishly "faithful" to someone who might well be dating another girl by now.

The night before he left, Daniel took me on a thrilling high-speed midnight ride on the back of his Vespa, from the Place de la Concorde down the Boulevard des Champs-Elysées (with miraculously sparse traffic) to the Place de l'Étoile, then back to the Concorde.

The Boulevard was an iridescent stream of light on both sides, with the illuminated glory of the Arc de Triomphe straight ahead in the middle of the Étoile.

The Vespa leaned in as we circled it several times and then zoomed back to the Concorde, with a cool breeze whipping our faces and the street scene whizzing by in a blur. It was a magical evening, though we avoided openly acknowledging it was likely to be our last.

April flew by too fast, with a pile of assignments and the realization that final exam season would soon be upon us. In France, that was the make-or-break academic hurdle. But we were hardly immune to distractions.

When Marisol passed through Paris one day on her way to a weekend in Brittany with some friends, Shirley and I decided to hitchhike and meet them in Dinar, on the Atlantic coast. The drivers who picked us up this time were unusually helpful.

An English couple took us along on a tour of several quaint villages, dropping us off to explore the famous abbey of Mont Saint-Michel, said to be the prototype for Dumas' prison setting in *The Count of Monte Christo*. It became one of my all-time favorite places.

Built in a sandy estuary on a massive, steep rock that during high tide becomes an island, while low tide exposes a strip of land with a connecting causeway, the huge abbey, with a simple gothic church at the peak of the multi-layered fortress, was more than impressive. This little church was second only to Chartres in the impact it had on me. Both felt deeply sacred, hard to leave, and somehow familiar.

The abbey was surrounded by a compact village, where we waited over an hour for Mère Poulard's world-famous omelets. They were worth the wait, as was the whole meal. Sated and relaxed, we easily found a ride to Saint Malo, stopped to look for a while at the ocean waves crashing ashore, and then took the ferry across the bay to meet our friends in Dinar.

Riding the ferry reminded me of my first encounter with the Atlantic Ocean ten years earlier when I sailed to America as a little girl. I still wasn't sure which side of the Atlantic was my real home. At that moment I would have said, "Right here."

At Dinar we lazed on the beach until our friends arrived. It was too cold to go swimming, but Shirl went anyway while I climbed rocks. Marisol arrived in the afternoon with two attractive young men, soon joined by two girls and a third man, and we all spent a lively evening sampling Brittany's famous crêpes at several restaurants. The charm and friendliness of the Bretons we met made this brief taste of Celtic France a special memory.

We drove back to Paris with six of us squished into a Peugeot, but the merriment in the car compensated for any discomfort. By now we were accustomed to "sardine experiences."

The following weekend we were on the road again, to Amsterdam by way of Brussels, the site of the World's Fair that year. This time we squeezed into a yellow Volkswagen bug belonging to a Scotsman who was dating a friend of ours. She had called several days earlier, saying they were passing through Paris en route to Holland, and would we like to come along? Yes we would.

The World's Fair was interesting, but Brussels was packed with people as well as expensive, so we moved on to adorable Amsterdam, the "Venice of the North," a clean and cheerful city with an irresistible charm. The people were hospitable, flowers overran every inch of available soil and usable container, and the city radiated a homey quality that made me envy the children who were growing up there. But from our newly sophisticated point of view it lacked the verve, complexity, and passion of Latin cities.

After a whirlwind of tulip fields, windmills, and tidy villages full of red-cheeked children with alabaster skin, we sped back toward Paris, passing once more through the Fair-induced chaos of Brussels and barely escaping death by tram.

That near-calamity was sobering, and led our driver to immediately modulate his kamikaze driving style, which ironically had been what saved us. As the tram was turning straight into the right side of our car, instead of slowing for even a split second, he instinctively floored the gas and got us across the tracks out of its way with inches to spare. There was stunned silence in the car for a while after that, but the trip as a whole had been a huge, unexpected treat.

We were now less than a month from the end of the academic year when we would have to vacate our dorm rooms. Paris was in its full springtime glory, but we had to spend most of that romantic month studying for exams. Much of that took place in our "study hall" café next door and was always subject to distractions. Since most of the people who might have led us astray were in the same boat, however, it worked pretty well.

It was a month of completions and, with that, a month of imminent goodbyes—a bittersweet time of having such rich experiences to treasure for the rest of my life, yet having to say goodbye not only to the city and country I had come to love, but also to dear friends.

I found myself nostalgic about J-P now that departure was imminent even though he was no longer in my life. He had probably been the most likely candidate for a long-term relationship of all my male friends in Paris, but my return to the U.S. and unresolved relationship with TK made that unrealistic. I had been happy with simple friendship, with both of us free to socialize with whomever else we wished, but he finally insisted on more commitment than I could accept.

After that he had slowly withdrawn from the scene. Though his decision was totally warranted, I still missed our good times together.

At the same time, leaving Paris meant that our traveling trio had a whole exciting summer to look forward to. We had all, with varying degrees of difficulty, obtained permission from our parents to stay and explore Europe until August, contingent on our having a plan that was safe and sensible. Hitchhiking fulfilled neither condition—and they didn't even know the whole story about that.

After some daughterly persuasion, Annie's father agreed to finance a car for us to travel in, which we would sell before going home. The proceeds would be subtracted from the cost, and the difference shared three ways. That left the cost of gas, food, and camping, all relatively inexpensive. There were good, safe campgrounds all over Europe, and student discounts for just about everything. We convinced our parents it was doable.

That is how we acquired "Henrietta," our gray "tin can with wheels," otherwise known as a Citroën *Deux-Chevaux* (literally, "two horses"). She became our rolling home, storage bin and, in a pinch, sleeping quarters. The floor of this car was totally flat, and the seats could all be removed and lifted outside, making it possible to contort our sleeping bags in a way that allowed all three of us to fit on the floor. We didn't expect to exercise that option much, but it was reassuring to know it existed.

Henrietta did have limitations. She couldn't go uphill beyond a certain degree of incline, and slowed down even on mildly rising roads. Yet, to her credit, like a jeep, she could go across fields and unpaved roads with aplomb. With some pushing, we discovered she could even get herself out of ditches if necessary.

Arriving two weeks before departure time, she mostly sat around and waited while we grappled with exams and the human connections we had established that were about to be severed. I had barely driven in a city because of New York's convenient public transportation system, so I took some time to hone my skills by driving her around Paris, racking up a few hair-raising memories. A friend told me that if I became comfortable driving in Paris, New York would be a breeze. I hoped he was right.

Late May and early June passed in a whirlwind of study and relationship closures. A letter from Daniel arrived from Martinique, making sure that my decision to go directly back to America still stood. He had written earlier to suggest that I detour through Martinique to spend some time with him, and hoped that perhaps I would change my mind. It was tempting, but I couldn't. I knew it was time to respond with a final goodbye, which I did with very mixed feelings.

Even TK, on whom I had almost given up, wrote. He hadn't expected me to stay in Europe through the summer, and perhaps that worried him. Good, let him worry a little, I thought, but had to admit that no one else had really had a chance with me, even though I had sincerely wanted to be open to other relationships. Still, goodbyes with the people who had been a part of my life for a year were sad, especially because I would be unlikely to ever see more than perhaps a few again.

To my relief, the exams went well. The intense cramming had paid off. The last and hardest exam was art. I had done well on the written part, but the oral was more challenging. It involved picking two topics at random and expounding on them in depth, then being grilled.

We dragged ourselves to the Louvre by 9:30, only to wait till almost noon to be called. I hadn't been that nervous in a long time. But it went well considering how tough M. Serullaz was in his grading. He was a superb teacher whom the whole class admired, but we feared his intellectual rigor when it was directed at us.

Marty, Shirley and I had spent many days at the Louvre and Jeu de Paumes museums pumping relevant facts into each other's heads. I owed my success in the exam largely to them. Happily, they did well, too.

Marty was a good friend who hasn't been mentioned yet. He was an ongoing buddy and brother figure from our Sweet Briar group. We hung out often, and shared the secret practice of going for lunch at the American Embassy's employee cafeteria. No, it was not open to the public; visitors were screened at the door and had to have a good reason to enter. Being an American student was not a good reason.

Back in autumn, we had developed a craving for American hamburgers and milk shakes, and decided to see if we could get past the guard by pretending to work there. In a suit, carrying his attaché case, Marty looked every bit the young foreign-service officer. Shirl and I also dressed to blend in with other female workers, and the three of us walked confidently past the guard, immersed in lively "work-related" conversation. Nobody stopped us, so we went in and had our milk shakes and hamburgers. The prices were amazing, just what our budgets needed. After that, the guards just waved us in, "recognizing" us as embassy employees.

Consequently we ate there many times, mostly after our class at the Louvre, since we were usually hungry and it was just a short walk. Marty was definitely someone I would miss: a smart, generous, all-around good person who would be certain to succeed in life.

The hardest person to leave was Marisol, who came to Paris for a farewell visit. I liked and trusted her more than any other friend. She was always honest and supportive, seemingly content with her own life with no personal axes to grind—the one person I was sure to stay in touch with for many years to come. That was a consolation, but I would still miss her.

Before we packed Henrietta, stored what we couldn't take along with friends, and took off to explore Italy and the rest of France, we made sure our return sailings were confirmed, each of us on a different date and ship.

Happy to have wheels now, we spent the last few days catching tourist sights in the Paris area that we'd missed, including the palace of Versailles, where we had only walked in the gardens before while visiting friends. On Tuesday, June 16, 1959, after a farewell lunch with Francine and her mother, we took off via Chartres toward Mont Saint-Michel. Annie had not seen it yet.

It was a celebratory drive. We had successfully completed our formal Junior Year Abroad, Mount Holyoke would be happy with our grades, and we were now free for the next two months to roam anywhere Henrietta was able to take us. We had learned so much, absorbed so much culture, laughed often and uproariously, danced till the wee hours, and talked endlessly over innumerable cups of coffee about the problems of the world and how we would fix them someday.

We had also wrestled with questions of identity and what to do with our lives, perhaps more complex for me because my ancestral home had been wiped off the geopolitical map long ago. Even a short visit was not possible.

I had spent many lonely moments trying to envision my place in this world, an outsider wherever I went even when accepted and welcomed. Ever since leaving Tallinn, I had felt that I fit in nowhere. Yet, in some strange way, I was now beginning to feel that I could probably create a life anywhere I chose. France had shown me that. Though still nostalgic for my early childhood Eden, I began to imagine the possibility of a place in the future where I "belonged," a place that really felt like home.

I felt that place could easily be Paris, but although I was not ready to say that yet, I knew deep down that my adult life would unfold in America. That would mean recognizing the past year as a once-in-a-lifetime escape from the confinements of the "real world"– like a colt released from the barn to run free for a while before being harnessed to carry an adult load of yet unknown weight.

Becoming a pseudo-adult at age six had shaped my growing years, and braving on had become a habit. The year in Paris had been a chance to feel what it was like to be unfettered and playful, to open my mind to intellectual and human vistas more exciting than anything I could have imagined. Sampling such a banquet of experiences as much as I could, while I could, felt almost gluttonous, but I would not have traded this time for anything.

And the incredible bonus of a summer odyssey was just beginning.

Chapter 29

INNOCENTS ABROAD

We dropped Annie off at the approach to the Abbey of Mont Saint-Michel and agreed to return in three hours. Shirl and I went looking for a local lunch place, a simple one with a fixed-price menu. Such menus tended to be limited, but in our experience the food was always excellent.

Determined to avoid the tourist areas, we drove to a quiet village nearby. Meandering through the side streets, we spotted an old stone building with "Restaurant" in faded letters over the entry, and a *prix fixe* sign posted next to the door. Exactly what we were looking for. We entered a bar area with a divider wall topped with plants to the left, just tall enough for the dining room to have privacy. When we told the man behind the bar, who turned out to be the owner, that we were there for lunch, he looked startled.

"Lunch?" he said as though asking a question.

"Yes. And you advertise a fixed price meal. How much is it?"

"Marie," he shouted to the woman behind a cash register toward the back, "These *demoiselles* want to have lunch. What is the price?"

Marie looked startled but quickly responded with a reasonable sum. We said fine. She came and hustled us through an entryway into the main dining room, seating us at a table for two against the opposite wall.

Content to have found what was obviously a local neighborhood hangout, we asked for the menu. She said they only had one option and rattled off what it included, adding with a subtle note of eagerness:

"If the young ladies would like more choices, I would be glad to refer you to some good restaurants in the center of town." I guess they're not fond of tourists, I thought, and replied that their menu sounded delicious.

She seemed a bit disappointed, despite an effort to appear welcoming. As we settled in to wait for our food, we looked around and noticed that everyone in the restaurant was staring at us, either directly or obliquely. A half dozen girls, perhaps sixteen or seventeen, filled a long table next to the entry. While eating they whispered among themselves, giggling and covertly looking in our direction.

Guess they're not used to foreign visitors, I thought.

A handful of men, who seemed to know each other, sat at several small tables like ours. They made no effort to hide their interest in us. Communicating under our breath in rapid English we hoped no one would catch, we decided to feign cluelessness about being the center of attention and enjoy our meal. The price was too good to pass up.

Our curiosity was aroused when two men got up and each signaled to one of the girls, who then followed them past the entryway to the bar section, and turned left rather than right toward the exit. When the same scenario was repeated, it occurred to us that this was odd.

"Can you see where they went?" I whispered to Shirley.

"Through the door with a beaded curtain behind the cash register."

"Are you thinking what I'm thinking?" Light was beginning to dawn.

"What do you mean?"

"Remember the article we read in *Le Monde* about training places in the provinces? They're young enough. It fits the story."

We tried to look normal. No wonder the customers had stared at us through the whole meal with half-smiles plastered on their faces. We were in the process of having a delicious home-cooked meal in a brothel. Who could ever have imagined this? Each time a new person walked into the "restaurant," he or she did a double take and rushed to someone already there to have a whispered exchange, with sideways glances at us. We felt like goldfish being ogled from all sides.

Now we had a hard time keeping a straight face. With great effort, we remained "oblivious," but it took gritty determination to contain ourselves while everyone else was enjoying a good laugh at our expense.

We finished eating, paid for our meal, did not ask to use the bathroom we assumed was somewhere behind the beaded curtain, and walked out—to the sound of uproarious laughter erupting behind the divider wall as we hastened to the exit. Once outside, we laughed our way back to the car to go pick up Annie, who was waiting for us.

"Sorry you had to kill so much time because of me," she said, "did you at least have a good lunch?" Then, seeing our faces, "What's so funny?"

Another burst of hilarity. "Oh, yes, it was *extraordinary.*"

Annie looked bewildered, and we relished telling our story. What a start to our summer.

Events unfolded rapidly. Every day was new, every discovery a revelation, every new person a one-of-a-kind encounter—and Henrietta rolling us through it all, her itinerary an *ad hoc* meandering along our general trajectory to a few pre-determined destinations. We had selected these city stopovers based on there being an American Express office, where we could pick up mail and allowance checks from home as well as cash travelers' checks.

There was one time early on when Henrietta's rolling became too real, and could have ended badly. We were camped for the night in a field on top of a cliff overlooking the sea, near Trégastel in Brittany. A magnificent sunset and a glass of wine had set the stage for a good night's sleep. Shirley and I settled in the car, Annie on the removed front seats outside under a makeshift tarp attached to the car's roof.

Next morning around sunrise, Shirl and I were jolted awake. The car was moving! Still half asleep, we realized it was rolling slowly downhill, toward the cliff that dropped down straight into the ocean.

Annie popped up from her "bed" when the tarp tore loose and fell on her. She was yelling at us while Shirley tried to untangle clothing from the steering wheel to turn it, and I scrambled to find the brake underneath the bulky sleeping bags. Luckily she managed to turn the car to a trajectory parallel to the cliff while I slowed it down and brought it to a stop.

We must have somehow disengaged the hand brake in our sleep. Whew! That was sobering. We decided that our sleeping arrangements needed an upgrade. We needed a tent, which would be easy to find in Tours, our next stop.

We had breakfast and drove on to visit Mme. Proust on our way south. She was as feisty and delightful as ever, giving us a local's perspective on some of the *châteaux* we had missed while limited to bicycle range during the time we lived with her. We enjoyed having her along, and she enjoyed the day with us. It had been a long time since she'd seen any of the tourist sights, as is often the case with people who live around "places of interest."

We all chipped in and bought a tent before we left Tours. It was a vast improvement. The tent felt cozy, safe from rain, and we rigged a flashlight to the pole to provide enough light to read and write by at night. Best of all, we could stretch our legs when sleeping, and there was enough space for four, which we would soon need.

We were going to Toulouse to pick up Lise, a friend from Le Foyer who planned to travel with us to the Riviera. But that was days away. We would be traveling through some of France's most beautiful countryside in the meantime, so there was no need to hurry.

Traveling leisurely now with the comfort of our tent, we absorbed the beauty of Dordogne and the stunning prehistoric caves at Lascaux, sheltered in lush, verdant countryside. Available to access only with a guide, these were the original caves, and being inside felt like a visceral bond across millennia with our ancient ancestors, with lives so different from ours yet so like us in their impulse to create enduring beauty through art.

The sense of awe stayed with us when we left to search for a camping spot. It smelled wonderful the next morning when we got up by the old château we slept near. Shirl made scrambled eggs and Annie oatmeal (our staple).

We drove through Périgueux with its Roman ruins and old quarters reminiscent of Spain. Our drive through Dordogne passed through the most beautiful countryside—greens of every shade, tall trees, rolling hills interspersed with little villages and red-roofed houses, while crystal-clear rivers and streams winding their way through the undulating countryside provided a great opportunity to bathe and do our laundry.

These were delightfully simple days, all with different sights, sounds, smells, and people. While in Toulouse for two nights to pick up Lise at her family home, we were happy to stay in a real house. A bed was more conducive to a good night's sleep than sleeping bags on the ground, we found, though being on the road was more exciting.

Continuing through the Pyrenees toward the Mediterranean, we passed deep grottos with cool streams and vivid green plains overflowing with wildflowers alternating with rocks, somewhat like the Alps, sometimes like the rolling hills I remembered from Estonia—each scene unique. Driving Henrietta over the winding roads was sometimes challenging, but so worth it.

We passed through Carcassonne—walking the medieval walled city for a couple of hours and having a meal—then down to Quillan where we found an exquisite camping spot beside an ice cold stream cascading down a mountain. The day ended celebrating Lise's birthday with a bottle of white wine.

The next afternoon we finally hit the coast at Perpignan. From then on, we hugged the shore as closely as possible, ending up on a beach near Béziers where we had another "Henrietta incident." The only cause of that one was our own stupidity.

We camped on a beach, parking Henrietta on what looked like well-packed sand, and pitched a tent next to her. Everything was lovely until it started to rain, then thunder with frightening cracks of lightning. We thought our tent's poles might be struck, and ran out clutching our sleeping bags.

Crouching outside next to a hut getting wetter and wetter, one of us had a bright idea. We went back to the tent and took out the poles. The tent collapsed on top of our heads. Shivering, we grabbed whatever sopping wet belongings we could, and ran into the car. It was one-thirty in the morning. Sleep was impossible, so we told stories and tried to have meaningful discussions. It felt like an endless wait till sunrise.

The storm having ended by daybreak, we tried to get out of the car, but couldn't. Our weight had caused the wheels to sink deep into the sand, including the bottom section of all four doors. We were hopelessly stuck.

Two fishermen finally found us, miserable and soaked to the bone. After joking with each other about the situation these *demoiselles* had gotten themselves into, they went and found some shovels to dig out the wheels, some flat pieces of lumber to put in front of them, and then managed to find some other men to help push us out.

Henrietta wouldn't budge. We tried to get her to help, but she only groaned and complained, though after the men dug out the doors as well, three of us could get out. The lightened load made it easier for them to push the car up the lumber strips while Annie steered. We also unloaded a lot of our stuff, which needed drying out anyway. Finally our dear abused Henrietta, now empty, found solid ground under her wheels on the paved road.

The first fisherman had also awakened the owner of a café down the beach to make us some coffee. Chivalry was not dead on the Mediterranean. Still wet and cold, we drank so much that we were no longer tired

Our unexpected breakfast gathering generated a lot of good-natured joking at our expense. What would possess anyone to drive a car onto sand, and then go sink it by adding a lot of weight, they pondered. We pled insanity. We told them they were our knights in shining armor, and we were so grateful to them for rescuing us and then providing breakfast. They laughed, but were obviously pleased.

We continued on to Marseilles, found a hotel, and went to sleep. Finally, the next morning, there was a chance to clean up, rest, and get re-organized. All our stuff was mixed up and damp.

Later, we went shopping for bathing suits—our first bikinis, a racy novelty for us since they were still unknown at home, considered too risqué for American morals.

Chapter 30

LA DOLCE VITA

Dried out and cleaned up, we continued on to Saint Tropez. After camping for one night, we decided to go on to Nice because St. Tropez was too Hollywood-glittery for us, not to mention expensive. Inspired by Brigitte Bardot's residing nearby, a lot of entertainment glitterati flocked there during the summer, creating a self-conscious display of glamor that spoiled an otherwise lovely town and perfect beach.

Somewhere on the coastal road, driving eastward toward Cannes after a splendid overnight on an almost deserted beach, with Henrietta on solid ground this time, we were still a bit sleepy and looking for a café to have our morning coffee. Shirley was driving, with me in the passenger seat, Annie and Lise both snoozing in the back.

On a stretch where there was nothing but beach on our right, with no buildings in sight, something suddenly caught my eye. What took shape as we approached was unreal. An Arab, complete with turban, was standing on the edge of the road, holding the reins of a camel (presumably his), and hitchhiking with his thumb out as we approached.

Shirl drove on without a word. I said nothing, knowing that I was awake but wondering whether I was still dreaming. I couldn't be hallucinating — could I?

After several minutes, Shirl asked in a casual tone, "Notice anything interesting along the road?"

I was not ready to commit to what I had seen. "An Arab?" was all I would venture.

"Hitchhiking?" She sounded relieved.

"Yes, but not alone." It couldn't be a hallucination. Two people couldn't have hallucinated the same implausible image at the same time, especially if she had also seen the camel.

"With a camel?" Shirley sounded cautious.

"Yes," I exclaimed, and we both laughed. We were not crazy after all.

Attempts to construct a plausible explanation for what he could have been doing there — camels in France were in zoos, not wandering around hitchhiking with their masters — hit a blank wall, and we finally gave up. After that, whenever one of us said or did something that made no sense to the other, the stock response would be: "And have you seen any camels hitchhiking lately?" It became our private joke, and remained an unsolved mystery.

We soaked up the sun on various beaches along the Riviera, then found a reasonable hotel in Nice and explored the town. The four of us strolled on the Boulevard des Anglais in our nicest summer outfits just for fun, blending in with the international tourist crowd, and Lise treated us to a farewell dinner. She was staying to meet some friends.

Going through Monaco on the way to Italy the next day, we spent the afternoon on a beach in Monte Carlo—in our new bikinis, of course, with well-developed tans by then—and decided to get to Padua by the following morning, then push on to Rome by the end of the day. We crossed the border to Italy after midnight and drove all night, taking turns at the wheel.

The sun came up after Genoa. We drove on mountain roads with hairpin turns, with mountain on one side and an impressive drop on the other. The view was breathtaking, but that stretch was too nerve-racking for us to fully appreciate it, more so for the passengers on the drop side than the driver. Nevertheless, we survived to arrive in Rome before dinnertime, found a hotel, and all dropped into our respective beds for a long sleep through the whole rest of the day until the following morning.

Perhaps influenced by the ambiance of relaxed Italian *dolce vita* (sweet life), we slowed down after that. Without any guidebooks, we meandered through the monuments and art treasures of Rome and the Vatican, took a cozy buggy ride through the Forum and Palatine Hill, and ate heartily in local neighborhood restaurants.

I contemplated Michelangelo's *Pieta* in St. Peter's for almost an hour, and was overwhelmed by the Sistine Chapel, so peaceful with only a dozen or so other visitors who silently shared our awe. I was deeply moved, even though I had rejected the Catholicism

I learned in high school. What I saw in Michelangelo's art was something way beyond that, in a way I couldn't express in words.

We could have stayed in Rome longer, but time was rushing by and we wanted to get down to Naples, especially to see Pompeii and Capri.

We drove to Pompeii first, in scorching heat that put a slight damper on our visit, but nothing could spoil the fascination of this ancient city where the past was even more alive than in Rome. Turning a corner, I could imagine meeting a gentleman in a toga who asked something like, "*Ubi Caius est?*" Walking where so many had walked so long ago, leading ordinary lives and suddenly being buried by Mount Vesuvius erupting, with no time to escape, felt simultaneously eerie, awesome, and unsettling. I saw Pompeii as a monument to life's fragility.

We had pitched our tent at a camp on the flank of that legendary mountain, complete with bubbling, boiling sulfur "sauna" caves reputed to be good for one's health. The smell was awful, but we had to try it. Actually, it did feel good afterward—perhaps just relief from the smell.

We didn't spend much time in Naples, except for a visit to the archaeological museum with its innumerable statues from Greek and Roman glory days. Instead we opted for the little island jewel of Capri, another tourist mecca but still with its own local character.

I had read a novel set at the Villa San Michele, the home of Swedish author Axel Munthe, when I was younger, and had dreamed of visiting Capri ever since. It did not disappoint. Perched at the tip of the rock that constitutes the island, the villa had an unsurpassable view of the Bay of Naples. About the house itself, I wrote in my journal:

> "I have no words to express what I feel. It (my ultimate fantasy home) has always existed in my dreams, but I would never have believed it could exist in reality. Yet there it was."

I didn't want to leave, and the little girl in me protested, "Why do I always have to leave places that make me happy?" But I was no longer a little girl.

We enjoyed our stay in Capri so much that we missed the last ferry to the mainland, but we were glad to stay the night once we located an acceptable hotel. Capri was a fairyland when illuminated. We left very reluctantly the next morning, vowing to come back someday.

Henrietta, parked at the dock in Naples, had survived our absence. Tired, we headed back to camp, intending to stop at a beach on the way, but took a wrong turn somewhere and found ourselves driving to the top of Mount Vesuvius on a narrow winding road with no turnoff and no safe way to turn around. As we ascended, the view of the whole bay and the beach we had been aiming for was glorious, but all we could do was look longingly at the water we had hoped to cool off in.

After finally arriving at a parking area near the top, we took a creaky old chairlift to the edge of the crater, emitting gurgling noises, puffs of smoke, and at the very top, a fantastic echo mocking our every sound.

The drive had been intense, the chairlift even more so, but what we saw was awesome. We deeply felt our human vulnerability in the face of Nature as we peered into the gurgling womb of the indomitable force that had once destroyed all human civilization within the range of our view.

The drive downhill was no less intense. Needing rest, we found our way back to camp, relieved that our tent and its contents were still intact. Knowing that the following day would be our last in southern Italy before returning to Rome and then France, we relaxed for the rest of the day and enjoyed a sulfur sauna at bedtime.

We decided to spend our last day in low-key Ischia, Capri's "wallflower" sister island, rarely visited by tourists in spite of its near-equal beauty. The ferry ride itself was worth the trip. We planned to be back early enough to get some good sleep before heading for Rome the next morning, but that didn't happen.

We missed the last ferry again, but this time it was deliberate. We had met two Italian students from Naples on the beach, with a third soon appearing out of nowhere—nice, attractive young men without the pseudo-romantic intrusiveness we were so used to dealing with in Italy. They were polite, intelligent, and we enjoyed their company. They wanted to take us to dinner and dancing in the evening and talked us into staying overnight, offering to pay for our room at a hotel near the friends they were visiting.

We had tentatively paired up, and I really liked
Franco, an intelligent, poetic soul who loved to sing.
My friends liked the others, too, so we were not hard
to convince. We all spent a long time singing on the
beach as the sunset panorama unfolded, and Franco
taught me the words to *Volare* and *Ciao, ciao, bambina,*
two popular Italian songs.

It was a sweetly intimate evening, walking on the
moonlit beach in the wee hours, talking about literature and life and future dreams in a way that I hadn't
with anyone for a long time. If things had been different, I knew we would have continued to see each
other, but as it was, that day was all we had, which
made it all the more precious.

The next morning, after breakfast together, all six
of us took the ferry back to Naples, where we three
had to hurry in order to return to camp, pack up, and
get to Rome by evening. We were now at the final
destination of our intended itinerary. It was time to
go back, with still so much to see, but now our ultimate destination was Le Havre, and the return voyage to America.

For me, there was still a half-dreaded piece of
unfinished business to complete. Our romantic day-
and-night in Ischia had been a perfect way to mark
this turning.

Chapter 31

SPECTERS OF THE PAST

Exhausted by the time we got to Rome, we settled into a hotel near the Pantheon, showered, and went to bed. Having beds felt luxurious, and we didn't budge again till noon the next day.

In high spirits, we headed first to American Express where at least one of us would hopefully find a check in the mail. We were out of money, except for what we needed to pay for our good night's sleep. We would move to the camp we had located on the outskirts of Rome as soon as we could.

While we were waiting in line, an attractive middle-aged man walked up to us and, after a polite greeting, asked if we would like to work for the day in a movie. Yeah, right. No, he was serious, he said, handing us a card with his name and "Titanic Studios" in big letters. They needed extras for a scene they were shooting, and we fit the bill. It wouldn't pay much, 4000 lire each, he explained apologetically, but we would get a free hair styling, a good lunch, and have fun. We said we'd come and check it out, still dubious. We could sure use the money.

The offer turned out to be legitimate. Shooting the same scene over and over was not terribly exciting, since all we had to do was sit in a mock airplane and act like passengers. All I had to do was say thank you when the "stewardess" handed me a cup of coffee. But the lunch was ample and delicious, spiced with laughter and racy gossip about the local movie scene, especially some of Victor Mature's antics. That caught my attention because his was the one name I recognized.

At the end of the day, we accepted an invitation to join the cast and crew for dinner and cocktails, not realizing what we were getting into. It turned out to be a bit much for us. We realized how naïve we were about movie world mores and excused ourselves as early as we could without insulting our hosts, on the grounds of leaving the next morning for Nice.

That was partially true. It had been our plan, but we decided to stay another day now that we had earned some money. Good sleep for two more nights would be a treat.

Before we headed north toward Florence, we tried to cover all the major sights recommended by the American Express tour desk, ending with claustrophobia in the Catacombs. The weather was scorching, so we tried to avoid full sunlight—except for making sure to throw the traditional wish-fulfilling coins in the Fountain of Trevi to assure our return someday.

Back at the hotel, we assembled a simple meal from market ingredients, packed, then strolled around the Pantheon neighborhood to absorb the evening ambiance for the last time.

Next morning we said *arrivederci Roma,* and reached Siena in time for a late lunch. We liked it too much to leave right away and didn't arrive in Florence until eleven that night. We had a hard time locating the camp we had chosen for our stay, but, even driving through the city at night, we were captivated by what we saw. That feeling grew by the hour the next morning when we went to explore it in daylight.

"There is a general harmony and artistic unity to the city that I haven't seen anywhere else, except for Paris," I wrote that night, "with little nooks and crannies everywhere sheltering artistic masterpieces. This city is a living museum of art—art as a part of it, not just something displayed for an elite ... the beauty of Michelangelo's *David* struck me dumb."

So did the Uffizi Gallery and all of Florence. I wondered what it might have been like to grow up in the midst of such a cornucopia of timeless art. It probably would have seemed ordinary to such a child.

The last day in Florence was dedicated to shopping for gifts to take home, as well as some for ourselves, since we had seen nothing like the esthetic quality and affordability of elegant leather goods, shoes, and scarves anywhere else. When we left, our gift lists were checked off—little things, but picked with care for each recipient.

On the way to the French border, we stopped at Portofino for a swim, so pleasant that we stayed too long and didn't make it across the border in time to find available lodging. Crossing this border in the middle of the night was becoming a habit, so we just pulled off the road near Monte Carlo and slept in the car. Quite well, actually—amazing what fatigue can do.

We settled into a camp between Nice and Cannes for the next five days. We had passed through this area quickly on our way to Italy, and now we set out to explore it in more detail, with our tent as home base.

> "The tent is fairly comfortable now," I wrote, "and the people here lent us three straw mattresses to put on the ground. Dinner was Annie's 'special'—beans, potatoes, and mushrooms cooked into a stew of some kind. Not bad, and certainly filling.... Discovered a gorgeous beach in Monte Carlo: turquoise cold, clean, clear water, a rocky beach and bright blue sky, looking up at a steep mountain dotted with a few white villas. We are getting tanned under this blazing sun, but not thinner since we depend mostly on bread and—when we can cook—some version of oatmeal, potatoes, and beans. Add some cheese or sardines for protein, and that's pretty much it."

Exploring artsy Vallauris and Aix along the way, we headed to Avignon for the summer festival of TNP, a major Paris theater ensemble. Marisol had given me contact information for the person with keys to a small place their family owned there, which she said we were welcome to use.

What a blessing! It was a cute little cottage, obviously not occupied for a while, which we cleaned up and made homey. We loved it. We settled in quickly and went to a play every night of the festival, thanks to France's student discount for all cultural events. Our IDs were still valid.

Wherever we went, the people of Provence were exceptionally kind. One day while exploring further afield, it became too late to drive back to Avignon. We couldn't find either a hotel or a place to camp, and stopped to ask a farmer's wife for advice. She took us home with her, put us up overnight in a storybook farmhouse with a beautiful view, and fed us breakfast the next morning before sending us on our way.

Perhaps she felt protective of three foolish girls wandering in foreign lands on their own. Or could it be that it is fundamentally more natural for us humans to act from our kind hearts than from our suspicious minds, contrary to what we are often led to believe?

It was in our cottage "home" in Avignon that I turned twenty-one, our modest celebration a fitting culmination to a joyful, carefree summer and a whole transformative year about to end. My remaining time would be solitary.

I was ready now to return to Germany to revisit Augsburg and my postwar childhood. I felt a need to see the site of the camp again through adult eyes. What if we had been stuck there until the camp closed? What if Uncle Gus had not entered our lives so miraculously? What would have become of us?

I knew this add-on journey would be financially challenging. I only had about thirty dollars in my purse when I left Shirl and Annie in Nice, and there would be no camping option. My father had arranged for me to stay successively with two of his old friends, both Estonian refugees who had found postwar jobs with the American military, one in Munich, close enough to Augsburg for an easy day trip, the other near Stuttgart, with a direct train connection to Paris. Train travel was very cheap for students.

If all went according to plan, my funds would last until Paris. Annie and I had agreed to reunite there for our final two weeks before departure. Shirley would already be back in the States.

It was sad to wave goodbye to both of them as my train pulled away from Nice, dismantling our traveling trio. Although that moment had been coming ever closer, the full reality now surprised me with an embarrassing flood of tears and a queasy, empty feeling in the pit of my stomach.

That train was taking me away from the most liberating, abundantly joyful year of my life, and now I had to return to the still unanswered questions that had haunted me since my visceral confrontation with human evil at age six. What is this life about? Where do I belong? Could I reconcile the senseless suffering I had witnessed with the incredible kindnesses I had received from so many benefactors? I hoped that this pilgrimage to the past would somehow bring some clarity.

I was groggy when my father's friend Mr. K met my train in Munich the next morning. I had not been able to sleep until two Italian men in my compartment got off in Switzerland, after talking and singing to me the whole time since leaving Genoa.

Mr. K and his wife turned out to be lively, fun, and very easy to be with. Two "honeymooners" who had been at it for decades, they were a welcome example that romance can survive a long marriage. What I saw in their union was my greatest dream for the future.

When they had to leave on a long pre-planned trip, I was disappointed to cut short this unexpectedly inspiring visit. They had arranged for me to stay with some friends, but it felt awkward after the first day. They were nice, but their efforts to entertain me allowed no solitude for sorely needed reflection time, so I left and went to Augsburg earlier than planned. Since paying for a hotel would wipe out almost all my remaining funds, I had intended to make it a day trip.

Finding affordable lodging seemed hopeless, but luckily a local resident directed me to an affordable bare but clean room in a family guesthouse near the city center, where I settled in for three days.

I decided to take the first day to orient myself and just wander around the city center. It felt strange to be back there after ten years—then a traumatized child, now a freshly minted adult. On the evening of the second day, which was spent revisiting the places I remembered, I wrote:

"I went to visit Hochfeld (where the DP camp had been) today. I took the #4 tram and got off at the cemetery, just before the long stretch that goes to Haunstetten. It hasn't changed much—the church is there, and the big chestnut tree I used to climb, only it isn't quite as big as I remembered. The Sunday School hall is transformed back into a *Gasthaus*. They have taken down the stone wall fence in front of the former schoolhouse, and also in front of the buildings on the street with the 'castle' where we loved to run and play catch. I even tried roller-skating on top of that wall.

"The metal bar across from the big square yard where I used to swing was still there, but there was grass instead of wood piles, and they had removed the big stones that used to separate our entry to Firnhaberstrasse 35 from 33. Someone named Jakobs lives in our apartment. The old kindergarten sandbox is still there.

"I had the urge to buy something at the bakery in the Latvian section, and ate two cheese pastries as I walked down our old hill (also smaller than I remembered) across what is no longer the field across which Mother ran into Father's arms when he found us after the war. It is now covered with a giant housing project.

"I reached the old station, still the same, walked in the woods (our crater with the tree across no longer there), visited the zoo, meandered through the outdoor theater and St. Ulrich's church. Passed the puppet theater and the Rotes Tor.

"I didn't take a single picture, despite my prior intentions. It is better so. It was a day for

memories, and deeply facing the stark reality
that nothing lasts. It is even hard to believe
that this was the place most like home during
our years in Germany. I have never had such
an overwhelming sense of rootlessness."

I spent the next day alone in my room, desolate,
letting my mind ride a carousel around life's unsolved mysteries and my unknown future. It rained
all day, as though Nature were shedding my unshed
tears for me. Then a poem wrote itself:

I am faced with a blank piece of paper.
I gaze at a bleak, crumbling wall.
What am I to write on this paper?
What am I to see on that wall?

I am bathed in warm golden sunshine,
I tiptoe on green, dewy grass.
What am I to feel in this sunshine?
How am I to tread on this grass?

I am facing a road leading nowhere
while sensing a compelling urge
to follow that road till it's somewhere
and then with it totally merge.

I want to know why and wherefore
these things evoke feelings in me
as though they had purpose, and therefore
would give me the courage to be.

There was something poignantly satisfying about anchoring my mental muddle in words. Even though the answers I had come back to find were as elusive as ever, I was glad I had come. Something felt complete. Whatever I had wanted to reconnect with no longer existed, yet its non-existence somehow opened up a future that was, in its unfathomable mystery, full of possibility.

Chapter 32

LETTING GO

I left the next day knowing my visit there was complete, took the train to Stuttgart and stayed for a few days with my father's other friend and his wife—warmhearted elders who did their best to show me around and entertain me with stories about their younger days in Estonia—until it was time to return to Paris.

Needing more time alone, I impulsively left a day early, even though Francine's mother, who had invited us to stay with her in Versailles, was not expecting Annie and me until the following day. I figured I would call her when I arrived and see if it was okay to come that evening instead. I was sure she'd say yes.

Unfortunately the train arrived much later than expected, and I found myself at the Gare du Nord in Paris close to eleven in the evening. It was very dark. I was a little wary of being alone at such a late hour in an unfamiliar neighborhood with a suitcase too heavy to carry very far. Moreover, I didn't know of any hotels nearby that I'd be able to pay for, and it was too late to call Madame and go to Versailles. In any case, there were no trains running at that hour.

While I waited for a bus to take me to a more familiar section of Paris, a pleasant man I had barely noticed who had shared my compartment on the train for most of the trip, walked by and asked if I would like to share a taxi. Taxis were not easy to find at that hour so I said yes, and asked if he knew a clean, reasonable hotel to recommend nearby.

Realizing that I was alone and essentially stranded, he offered his apartment as an option, assuring me that there was no improper motive involved. He said his ten-year-old son was away at camp and I was welcome to use his room for the night. There was something about him that I trusted, and I had no other viable option, so I gratefully accepted.

His apartment in Montmartre was within a stone's throw of the famous Moulin Rouge nightclub, its multicolored lights flickering on his living room wall opposite the window. We had a late-night snack and talked for several hours.

My host turned out to be a well-known movie director and actor. The mother of the son whose room I was borrowing was a famous French actress I admired. They were divorced. As a theater and movie buff, I found our conversation exhilarating, and we continued the next morning over coffee. When it was time for him to leave for work, he said I was welcome to stay as long as I needed to, and gave me a card with his phone number. In case I decided to leave, he showed me how to lock the door as I went out.

He left with my heartfelt thanks for materializing the night before as my "white knight" — how appropriately theatrical. Since I was committed to going to Versailles to meet Annie, and there was still much wrapping up of the year to do, I couldn't accept his generosity. I wished we had met earlier during the year, when there would have been time to get better acquainted.

When I arrived in Versailles, Madame welcomed me graciously and, after getting me settled in the guest room, pointed to a letter on the nightstand. Marisol, who she said could not be reached, had mailed it to Versailles, knowing I would receive it when I returned to Paris. I expected a short note saying *au revoir* and bon voyage, so when I opened it, the last thing I expected to read was: "This is the last time I will be writing to you, or anyone..."

She was about to enter a cloistered religious order to devote her life to prayer and contemplation. That meant she would be renouncing all contact with the outside world. She was happy, she wrote, and had been contemplating this decision for several years. She would remember me in her prayers, wished me a wonderful life, and told me to remember our friendship and the good times we'd had together.

I was speechless. I knew she must have given it a lot of thought, but she had never shared that part of herself. I had felt her deep and genuine spirituality in the way she lived her life and related to people, but this was a shock.

I could understand her becoming a nun, having known several with her humor and exuberance, but a silent recluse behind cloister walls? I simply couldn't picture her in that setting, not for the rest of her life. I tried hard to be happy for her but mourned the end of a valued friendship, at least in its external form. Inwardly, I knew I would treasure her luminous spirit and never cease wondering how her life as a nun unfolded.

On the pretext of wanting a final stroll in Versailles, I went for a solo walk in the palace gardens to shed my tears in private.

Annie arrived the next evening with trusty Henrietta, which we now had only a week to sell. She was too tired to unpack the trunk, which held all the gifts we had accumulated over the summer. We figured it would be safe to leave them in the car in a neighborhood off the tourist track.

The next morning, the trunk was empty. All our carefully chosen gifts were gone, and it was too late to replace them. Being robbed was a shock. It brought us back, after a perfect summer, to the reality of malevolence in the world.

We managed to sell Henrietta to a friend of a French friend just before our time was up. Our last days in Paris were a runaround of errands and completions, last croissants at a favorite bakery, and coffee with whichever friends happened to be in Paris at the time. Last bits of sightseeing, too, in case we had missed something.

The reality of leaving seemed unreal. I felt a deepening sense of loss, almost mourning, which made no sense given that I was returning home to my beloved family, a college I loved, and a boyfriend I had missed all year who had finally written to wish me a happy birthday.

The last night before taking the train to Le Havre to board the *Queen Elizabeth* was magical. Annie and I were sitting at Le Bac, our "study hall" café, sipping a final glass of wine. We started conversing with a man who lived practically around the corner, but whom we had never met before.

François was a journalist, attractive and intelligent, and we hit it off. Because it was our last night in Paris, he drove us to several of our favorite spots to say farewell. Annie had to go at some point, leaving François and me to meander around Paris for much of the night, talking in unexpected depth and regretting that we hadn't met earlier. How ironic that we had lived so close to each other all year, felt such spontaneous rapport, and yet never met until my last night in France.

The air was brisk, an early warning of autumn's approach. Walking on the Right Bank of the Seine, home to a number of *clochards* (homeless people), we saw that one man camped under a bridge had made a fire and asked him if we could warm ourselves.

He said yes, and we talked with him for a long time. He turned out to be a well-read fireside philosopher with a bent for trenchant commentary on the life he observed from his vantage point on the river. My companion finally asked him why, given his obvious intelligence and knowledge, he was living as he was. He smiled and looked directly into our eyes, in turn. *"Moi, je suis libre,"* he said. *"Et vous?"* (I am free. Are you?).

He was the City of Light's last gift to me, as was François—an anonymous neighbor who appeared out of nowhere to companion and protect me on this farewell night in my beloved city. Our brief time together was poignant, and I held its memory close as I hurriedly finished packing at dawn, took a brief nap, and barely made the boat train—with a lump in my throat and holding back tears.

On the first evening of the journey back across the Atlantic, I wrote in my journal: "*Adieu jeunesse, la liberté! Bonjour tristesse, responsabilité!*" (Goodbye, youth and freedom! Hello, sadness and responsibility!). I knew that was melodramatic, but it reflected a deep sorrow over something very precious that was over—a year of being authentically myself, capped by a magical summer, as though stepping out of time into an alternate reality of free flow and limitless options. It had been a dream from which it was time to wake up, but it would always be a part of me.

I tried to console myself with the idea that if I wanted to, I could return to France after graduation, but knew it was unlikely. And probably just as well. I had heard or read somewhere: "Never try to repeat a perfect experience."

Chapter 33

HELLO AGAIN

The *Queen Elizabeth*, flagship of the Cunard Line, was the largest passenger liner on the Atlantic. I cocooned myself for the five days of crossing either in my state-room in the bowels of the ship ("student class"), on a deck chair in good weather, or a cozy sofa in the lounge when stormy. I emerged three times a day for meals and once or twice for an evening movie, but chose solitude the rest of the time.

Most of the people on board were friendly but older. The "Queen Liz" had a reputation for being relaxing and dignified, or staid and boring as my generation saw it. However, boring was good for my purposes. I needed time for quiet reflection, to catch up on sleep and prepare myself for reentry into a life that had begun to feel distant. I felt resistance to stepping back into a matrix of social expectations and limitations, and was grateful to have that five-day window of time to shift gears.

I thought a lot about my parents, and the sacrifices they had made to allow me to stay in Europe for the summer. They had increased my allowance although the family was living close to the bone, even with both of them working full time. My father's whole life had been nothing but study and work.

The oldest of five children who took on a lot of responsibility after his mother died just as he entered his teens, he had grown himself from rural school-master's son to distinguished educator and head of the Tallinn Technical Institute, with a beautiful wife and daughter who delighted him—only to have it all swept away. When World War II forced them into exile, he was forty-six and "at the top of his game."

With everything in his past suddenly wiped away, he had found himself stranded in the midst of war, responsible for a small child and a pregnant wife, as well as a feisty mother-in-law. He had worked so hard for the life he had created, and now it was gone, including the role of respected teacher.

He had loved teaching, loved his students, and they loved him. Would he ever again be able to express that part of himself in his work? The difficulty of a new language in which he could not yet adequately express himself ruled that out when he came to America, except within the Estonian émigré community. Being older than fifty was also an issue. Regardless, he was willing to do whatever necessary to support his family, and he did everything he took on with impeccable diligence and dignity.

The possibility of anything like the kind of free-dom he had just made possible for me had never existed for him. Yet, with true generosity, he delight-ed in my academic achievements and always did everything he could to support my expanding interests even if they were silly at times.

He had always treated me as someone worth listening to and taking seriously, even as a small child, and as I grew older we had wonderful conversations about philosophy, religion, science, politics, and much else. He relished my taking ideas seriously, and was willing to engage in debate when called for. I was always free to disagree with him as long as I could make a good rational case for my view, based either on facts or on authentic personal experience.

Perhaps his greatest gift to me was his open-mindedness. In his own way, he was a visionary. He never conveyed in any way that my being female limited anything I might aspire to. Yet I always knew that he hoped it would be something to benefit the world, though he never said that explicitly. Far ahead of his time, he was both religiously ecumenical and globally aware, caring deeply about what happened in the wider world beyond his own people and interests.

I never heard him say anything derogatory about any group as a whole. For him, there were no "they" who were wrong and "we" who were right. There were only diverse individuals with different personalities and viewpoints, some preferable to others.

I had always taken our intellectual father-daughter give-and-take for granted as normal, and his goodness as a given. Having grown into a wider perspective and learned about friends' relationships with parents, I had come to realize that what for me was normal was not the norm for everyone. That raised my respect and gratitude for being the daughter of this extraordinary "ordinary" man.

Mother, whose father had died when she was a baby, had been raised in far greater material comfort, due to Mamma's independence and resourcefulness as well as support from her older siblings. She married quite young, at twenty-one, perhaps looking for the father she never had.

She was twelve years younger than he, and spent their first seven years creating a beautiful home and engaging in social and cultural activities in Tallinn. That was the kind of life she had enjoyed most, making her heroism during the war unexpected.

She also loved to travel, which Father's mounting professional responsibilities made difficult. He recognized that her youthful energy needed more outlets than he could share, and encouraged her to travel on a family ship captained by her brother-in-law, with her childhood buddy Sigrid as companion (technically her niece, but close to her in age because of a two-decade gap between Mother and her sister).

She took full advantage of this opportunity, cruising to foreign cities such as Helsinki and London. She wanted to have fun for a while so that when she decided to have children, she would be ready to settle down and devote herself to motherhood. During her travels, she decided that if her first child is a daughter she would call her Hillevi, a name she ran across during one of her voyages.

When I was born, I became the center of her life. She was a passionately devoted mother. I remember sitting on her lap in a rocking chair by the window, waiting for Father to come home while she sang to me and read stories. I loved our dining room, with its shiny mahogany table, high-backed chairs, shiny parquet floor, and a glass-front cabinet holding china and crystal. I was encouraged to participate in din-nertime conversation, even with guests, which taught me to take my turn without interrupting. I realized I had been born into an ideal situation.

Mother lost a second child, a boy, to a miscarriage during the first Russian occupation in 1941, possibly due to the trauma of the occupation and mass depor-tations to which she lost her sister and other family members. When she became pregnant again, she de-termined to carry the baby to term no matter what, in spite of the rapidly deteriorating political situation. While several of her friends chose to end their preg-nancies (medical abortion was legal in Estonia), she could not bring herself to do it.

The importance to her of this baby made it even harder to leave her whole life behind and flee to an uncertain future so close to term—yet all the more imperative.

Looking back at this legacy on the *Queen Elizabeth* as an adult, I couldn't imagine what my parents must have gone through in those tragic days, and marveled at their courage. Their inner strength throughout the exodus from their home, and the harrowing events that followed in exile, now filled me with awe. Could I ever live up to such examples? I didn't think so, but I could try to achieve some of their unrealized goals if I could.

I also thought about what I had left behind in France, including the seeds of an imagined future life, and relationships I had walked away from—memories that already felt less real than just a few days ago. Reflecting on the magic of the past year against the background of my family's history and the reality of our life in America made it clear to me where my future lay. Yet, in the immortal words of Ingrid Bergman in *Casablanca*, I too would "always have Paris."

I wondered what it would be like to be with TK again. I was eager to see him, though deep down still unsure about his steadfastness in marriage over the long haul. His anti-conventional, idiosyncratic personality had attracted me, maybe because he challenged my always having been careful to stay within acceptable social norms, but it also made me wonder how he would manage the roles of husband and father.

To me, marriage had always implied children as a matter of course, though I was no longer as certain about that as I had been. My mind had opened to so many other possibilities that future choices facing me felt more complicated now.

To lift my spirits and not show up in New York with a long face, I put together a poem about our trio's summer. It popped into my mind after hearing the ship's orchestra play the song "People Will Say We're In Love" from the musical *Carousel*.

Don't tell them what we did,
Don't tell them what we ate
Or why we drove so late –
People will say we were nuts.

Don't say the tent got wet,
Or how the fender bent,
Or where the money went –
People will say we were nuts.

They'll smile and shake their heads
Doubtful of all that we said,
But we're pleased with the life we led
Though people still say we were nuts.

Writing this cheered me up, and I began to look forward to our arrival. Senior year at Holyoke would be fun. With the year's curriculum in Paris, I had exceeded all the requirements for my major, which gave me wide latitude in selecting electives. I also looked forward to seeing friends and hearing about their year on campus.

Most of all, I was anxious to see my family, the one source of rootedness that I could always count on. Wherever I would roam, my parents would always welcome me home. It was *they* who were "home," not where they lived. Ultimately, home is where love is.

I knew that all I had seen and learned during my expansive, magical year could never be lost. It had been a year out of time, indelibly imprinted in my soul. Although the search for my ultimate, ideal home would likely continue, I had discovered in myself a capacity to make strong human connections wherever I went.

My worldview had expanded so much that I knew I could create a good life anywhere on this earth. I did not have to be either European or American.

I could be both and neither. I could always go back and visit Europe, perhaps some day even Estonia, but America was where I would root myself.

Finally, the New York skyline appeared in the distance. As I sailed toward Lady Liberty for the second time, she seemed to be waiting for me, holding her torch in welcome. My response was a surprising surge of euphoria.

A decade ago, she had been a portal to an unknown future. This time, I just smiled at her and murmured: "Hi Lady, I'm back."

Chapter 34

HAPPY EVER AFTER?

Before I could settle in at home, I found myself once more passing through Mary Lyon's gate to start my senior year, this time driven by TK. He had been at the dock to meet me when I arrived, and our relationship took off again in high gear.

To my delight, I found that many of my friends would be living in my dorm. As familiar as being back felt, everything was also different. I was seeing through different eyes. But the campus was as gorgeous as ever, and in a month there would be another New England autumn. The mountains around us would explode into a rainbow of multicolored hues and then, one random morning in October, the chapel bells would ring to announce Mountain Day.

We never knew when. All classes would be canceled, the dorm kitchens would supply picnic lunches, and we would all take to the mountains or wherever else Mother Nature called us. How I loved that tradition!

Yet my heart ached every time I thought of Paris, not any thing or any one in particular, just something

I missed terribly that felt gone forever. But I had made my decision, and I knew it was time to focus on the reality of now. My last year before "real life" truly set in had arrived.

Except for the yearlong course in human physiology, it became a year devoted to the arts: theatre, advanced French lit, sculpture, playwriting, music history, and an honors thesis. I had leading roles in several plays, smaller ones in others. As part of my honors work, I directed a contemporary one-act play in French as well as a full-length English Restoration comedy, *The Man of Mode*.

Directing was a real discovery. In some ways, I found it more rewarding than acting, and had a knack for it that surprised both me and my teachers. Understanding multiple characters and their interplay within the plot was more challenging than bringing just one character to life, I loved it. I didn't feel I could inhabit a role as fully as those with a real gift for acting can, yet I could more easily feel my way into the psyches of different characters and foster their embodiment on stage through someone else.

I therefore decided to aim for teaching and directing rather than acting as a more viable career path in theatre, probably in the context of an academic job. That may have foreclosed the acting option prematurely, but it was more practical and therefore reassuring to my parents, who felt (accurately) that acting was hardly a dependable livelihood.

Monsieur Saintonge and Miss Shepardson, my academic mentors, suggested that I continue on to graduate training at the Yale Drama School, which would lay the groundwork for teaching options. They encouraged me to apply for a Woodrow Wilson fellowship, a stipend that would pay my way to a doctorate. I doubted I had any real chance of success, but I could always withdraw if I changed my mind. There was no harm in trying.

Meanwhile, the relationship with TK gathered steam. The push for marriage got intense because, within the sexual mores of the time, a woman's choice was either marriage *or* career, with the assumption of virginity before marriage and "marrying well" as a mark of success, far preferable to a career.

The "career woman" image was still tinged with an "old maid" aura. On the other hand, Fifties' movies offered a contrary option: to marry for "love" and "live happily ever after" with someone sexy and exciting rather than the nice "boy next door." I had grown up enchanted with that romantic image, prematurely ruling out some fine young men who did not fit the bill.

TK, however, with his movie-star looks and blatant sex appeal, was a poster boy for Hollywood-style fantasies. If it had been socially acceptable for us to live together for a while first, our marriage might never have taken place, but with a testosterone-and-oxytocin haze veiling rational judgment, and people telling us what a "handsome couple" we made adding fuel to the fire, we got engaged on Valentine's Day.

The passionate urge to merge silenced any questions of whether we were ready for marriage, much less parenthood. To my naively romantic self, our

powerful attraction meant "true love," and therefore marriage. In addition, many of my classmates
were already engaged and making wedding plans,
swept into the "senior-year-girls-getting-engaged-to-
be-married-after-graduation" wave so prevalent in
women's colleges, and I swam with the tide.

We decided on a wedding two weeks after graduation, ignoring my parents' encouragement to wait
a few months before rushing into a lifelong commitment. It fell on deaf ears. Wedding plans became my
main focus, and supplanted the intention to make the
most of what remained of my time in college.

Another factor in the decision to marry TK quickly,
aside from compelling sexual attraction, was cultural.
Although my parents had unspoken but implied res-
ervations about him as a husband, father, and provid-
er (he had attended Princeton for five years but failed
to graduate—a long story), they were comfortable
with his being Estonian. TK's parents were very different from mine, but they came from the same eth-
nic background and spoke the same language, so he
would fit easily into our family. I ignored my parents'
qualms because, if I was to marry an Estonian, TK
was the one I could most easily imagine living with.

My parents' comfort was important to me, and I
knew how much they were looking forward to grandchildren. Since motherhood was a universal expecta-
tion for married women, I never asked myself if I was
actually suited for it. My mother filled the maternal
role with such natural ease (or so it seemed to me)
that I thought everything would come automatically
when needed, in spite of the fact that I knew nothing

about babies and had never spent any time with them even by babysitting.

I was taken with the media image of a happy family, and imagined a life that would reconstruct the memory of my idyllic early childhood. Somehow the fact that I was very different from my mother in personality and interests escaped my awareness. Though we shared a love of travel and the arts, she was totally devoted to family and close friends, while I was most strongly drawn to explore the human condition in all its diversity, inner and outer.

Through that spring, I coasted academically but managed to pull off decent grades, with one exception. One can't coast through an honors thesis, especially when approaching spring break without having given it much thought. It was a poor echo of my usual work, enough to kick me off the "highest" to "high" honors list at graduation, but I was too starry-eyed about the wedding to care.

I knew it was a disappointment to my mentors, who were still cheerleading my graduate school plans, and when I decided to withdraw from both the fellowship and application to Yale Drama School in favor of marriage, they were speechless.

I didn't blame them. For them, the fellowship had been a "done deal," and they saw a promising career in my future. They had put so much energy into mentoring me, and my graduating with "highest" honors would have honored their departments, too. I had clearly let them down.

I felt terrible about that, but what I felt even more strongly was a deep, visceral relief. That puzzled me.

Was my decision a copout, out of fear that I could not again "rise to the occasion" as everyone expected? Was I afraid that "the road less traveled" might create problems between TK and me at the very beginning of our marriage? Or perhaps the little girl in me still had illusions of reliving a childhood memory of happy domesticity.

Whatever the reasons, my choice was in sync with what women like me were expected to do: to marry "my man," become a devoted "educated housewife," have two or three children, and live America's ideal of the "good life."

I knew that my father was disappointed. As ever, he was gracious about my decision, but I knew that he felt I would be wasting my education. War had interrupted his life and aborted his fulfilling his own potential, so he had glowed with pride at my every accomplishment. I felt sad about that, but still clung to my decision.

Both parents drove up to Mount Holyoke with TK to attend graduation. It was the first time they had visited the campus. They loved it and delighted in all the ceremonies, especially Father. I had never seen him smile so much.

When I introduced TK to M. Saintonge at our French Department reception, it was obvious from the tone of his conversation with my future husband that Monsieur regarded him as the culprit who had enticed me off my destined path—to waste my talents as a mere housewife. He did make an effort to be gracious, but succeeded only at bare civility. I could tell that Miss Shepardson shared his feelings, but in her case it wasn't so obvious. She was a good actress.

Once home with diploma in hand, I plunged into a whirlwind of activity. I designed my own wedding dress, executed by the same talented woman who had made my high school prom dress. Mother handled the reception plans. TK was in charge of our arrangements for a honeymoon in Montreal and Quebec. I floated around in a pink cloud sprinkled with fairy dust.

When the big day arrived and I was getting ready to walk down the aisle on my father's arm, I had a sudden impulse to bolt, as in the movies when the heroine flees at the last moment to join the man she truly loves.

Surprised, I ignored it as mere bridal jitters. My "Prince" was waiting for me by the altar. There was no one else in the wings. What I had turned my back on was just a dream. Paris seemed distant now, and my life was here. I took Father's arm, the organ announced the big moment, and I floated down the aisle. No turning back now.

Once the qualms subsided and we were pronounced man and wife, I felt supremely happy, bursting with anticipation and hope for the future. The sunny sky over Manhattan was an unusually clear blue, which seemed like a good omen.

The little girl who had curled up behind her mother's mirror to fend off the inevitable, and braved on through war and exile to become an "uncommon woman" and world traveler, had now reached the magical moment that all little girls like me dreamed of, marrying the man she loved at a beautiful wedding in a beautiful dress.

I was Cinderella at the ball, dancing with my Prince Charming into our "happily ever after."

Afterword

Does anyone really live happily ever after? Perhaps. For us, the "honeymoon" lasted several years in spite of TK being drafted and our spending two years as an itinerant military couple.

Upon his discharge, while settling into suburban life and planning to have a family, the consequences of the decision I had made before graduation began to dawn. Why hadn't I taken more time before burning my academic bridges? Why hadn't I allowed life to unfold at its own pace?

Although I might have denied it even if I'd known it consciously, I had been afraid to leave the cultural cocoon that had been my lifelong security. I did not believe that my own wings would be strong enough to carry me in the wider world, so I sought security in marriage to a strong man who would take care of me.

I tried hard to be happy and create a comfortable, loving home, as I had seen my mother do in all kinds of circumstances. When our son Michael was born, he totally captivated me and delighted the whole family. I loved him, and I loved my husband, with all my heart—yet there was an empty hole inside. I was convinced I was depressed and consulted a local psychiatrist. After an hour, he said there was nothing wrong with me that learning to bake cookies and keep my husband happy in bed wouldn't cure. With a patronizing pat on the shoulder, he assured me it was just a touch of postpartum blues and would pass in no time.

His ignorance shocked me. I felt even worse. I immersed myself in psychology books, desperately trying to understand why I felt as though a part of me were dying when I had so much to be happy about.

Then Betty Friedan's *The Feminine Mystique* exploded into the culture and landed a bull's eye in my gut—she was writing about *me*. I was a poster girl for "the problem that has no name," an experience common in college-educated women who had bought into the idealized happy housewife myth. Feeling stifled and unfulfilled, but thinking there must be something wrong with us, we hid these feelings behind a cheerful façade.

I no longer felt odd and alone. We were legion, our problem was real, and there was something I could do about it.

Meanwhile, I had become pregnant again, hoping fervently for a girl to complete our family. Mother Nature complied, and Dominique's arrival brought a burst of sunshine with it. My parents doted on the little ones, and their delight in their grandchildren delighted me in turn. But I still felt that a part of me was dying.

To understand this, I read voraciously and began to realize that you cannot live successfully as someone you are not. To feed my mind, I entered graduate school to formally study psychology. After another series of fortuitous events led to a full graduate fellowship in the clinical psychology Ph.D. program at Columbia University, I matriculated in 1967 with two toddlers in tow and everyone I knew thinking I was out of my mind.

We moved into a cramped graduate student apartment while TK worked as a construction engineer on the World Trade Center site. For me, being a mother while a full time student in a demanding graduate program was challenging to say the least, but I loved it even though I felt like an outsider once more.

Women were a minority in psychology doctoral programs, and I was the only woman in my class who was both married and a mother. I wasn't sure I could make it through, but focusing on one day at a time, and with my still working parents' generosity in caring for the children during weekends, we made it work.

My internship took us to Honolulu, where we ended up staying for sixteen years. The early years were happy ones, and very busy, but we always took time as a family to enjoy the ocean and the breathtaking beauty of the islands.

After seven years, TK and I divorced and I became the sole support of the children while working as a member of the psychiatry department at a major Honolulu hospital. I loved my job, my patients, and the pioneering wellness program I was able to create there—a stretch for the prevailing mindset of the 1970s, but an early sprout of a trend that would soon spread everywhere. "The Healthing Center" integrated stress management and healthy lifestyle training with nutrition, exercise, and medical monitoring.

Hawaii's greatest gift to me, however, was spiritual. I still think of the Islands as the land of my "spiritual birth." It was a transformative time, launching an inner journey that would last a lifetime.

I remarried, and in time we relocated to the Bay Area, where serendipity led to my favorite working years, as core faculty at the Institute of Transpersonal Psychology in Palo Alto. There I did my best to pass on what I had learned to prospective psychologists and counselors. The most fun I had was teaching Jungian psychology and dream-work.

Single once more when almost retirement age—a divorce by mutual agreement due to diverging life paths—I plunged into Buddhist studies and practice, semi-retired to Southern Oregon, wrote a book, counseled people seeking psycho-spiritual wholeness, and became the grandmother of six beautiful children.

My youthful decision to renounce the dream of living in France, to back away from a possible future in theatre, and to marry an interesting man who was not "good husband material" in the conventional sense, all turned out to be parts of a tortuous path that eventually brought me to a happy autumn of life, with time at last to focus on writing.

Reflections

From my vantage point now, I can see the lifelong growth of early seeds planted through my family's war and postwar experiences. I can see that my lifelong aversion to black-or-white thinking and collective labeling grew from my six-year-old confusion about "good guys" and "bad guys," and from the shocking juxtaposition of good and evil that stopped me in my tracks on the church steps at age six.

I knew that Germans were responsible for the war that destroyed the life I had known, yet a German girl saved me from being bullied by her friends, and when we were hungry during our flight from the advancing Soviet army, German farmers often shared with us the little food they had. How could I say all Germans were bad?

The Americans to whose protection we fled were also the source of the gauntlet of bullets we had to survive in order to reach them, while Sarge and his cohorts threatened my mother with guns. Yet in the end it was Americans who housed and fed us, welcomed us to their country, and gave us a new life and me a first-rate education. Wrestling with such paradoxes led me at an early age to probe beyond appearances before judging or labeling. I learned from experience that any label we affix to a collective "they" is inherently false.

My mother, with a compassion and integrity that never wavered, repeatedly found a way through seemingly hopeless crises. She taught me by example that, no matter what, while there is life there is possibility. With her total focus on the raw reality of each moment, driven by a relentless resolve to live free, she braved on and somehow attracted the response of a benign fate that saved not only us but also two other families from the Gulag.

To me, she personified authentic feminine strength in action, and that has served as a pole star in my own life. She also modeled unconditional kindness, and demonstrated that striving for beauty and graciousness is possible regardless of external circumstances. I have never forgotten her wildflowers in tin cans during our seemingly endless walk to freedom.

The kindness of strangers at pivotal moments was an unexpected grace that followed and sustained our family even after settling in America. I feel protected by our benign "fate" to this day. Why that is so remains a mystery to me. I have tried to be kind in turn, knowing that we can never anticipate the potential benefits of simple kindnesses like those that ensured our survival.

I also learned something about fear during the war that changed the way I've related to it ever since: fear does not exist in the present moment. The thoughts that generate fear arise almost instantly, but they always relate to past or future: what should or could have happened, why it happened, what else I could have done, what more can go wrong, what did I do to deserve this, whose fault is it, and so on.

In the moment, however, there is only the stark reality of what *is* and how nakedly, spontaneously response-*able* we are. When my mother faced the soldiers' guns, there was no calculation in her response. Had she stopped to think, she might have wavered and we would have ended up on that truck.

It was the unconditional authenticity of her "No"—undiluted by forethought or fear—that paralyzed Sarge. He had no habituated response to that. When I asked Mother in old age about where her courage had come from, she seemed surprised at the question. "I did what I had to do," she answered, "any other mother would have done the same."

I believe we are always called to our authenticity. If we answer that call, the inevitable detours along the way become a teaching. Along such a journey, life will show us what we need to know, and a sustaining grace we may not have recognized earlier will become the wind beneath our wings. At least, that has been my experience.

Such grace works in mysterious ways. When I reflect on that long-ago call of the luminous Alpine mountaintop to the exhausted little refugee girl walking to save her life, I see that call as a pointer to what would become possible for her as her life unfolded, in ways that she could never have imagined. I am profoundly grateful.

ACKNOWLEDGEMENTS

It takes a village to raise a child, as the saying goes. It also takes a village to birth a book, and this one had many helpers along the way. I feel such gratitude to all of you for giving me your time, support, and feedback when what I had written needed an objective eye.

At the head of my cheering section was Berkeley Fuller-Lewis, a longtime friend and veritable twenty-first century "Renaissance man," ever available as a technical consultant and all-around sounding board. With skills ranging from graphic arts to writing to computer wizardry and marketing, he created the cover (with my kibitzing on the side) and served as a one-man support hub through the whole process. Thank you, Berk, so much.

To the pre-readers of *Under Fate's Wing* for their generosity and willingness to wade through various stages of an unfinished manuscript and make constructive comments, I extend my deepest gratitude: Valerie Atchison, Gretchen Bealer, Janet Germane, Mary Flett, Judith Millburn. Myra Reese, and Judy Timmel. A special thank you to Hal Bennett, who supported me early on and told me, when I wasn't sure myself, that I *must* write this story, and to Juris Jurjevics for some good suggestions and a needed wake-up call.

In the later stages when the "baby" was showing signs of imminent life, Bonnie Greenwell, Alissa Lukara, and Robin Seeley helped to refine the story further, and Marea Claassen pointed to a number of spots that needed fine-tuning. Thank you all so much for your efforts and loving support.

Finally, before entry into the "birth canal," Michael Kroon, copy editor extraordinaire, pronounced the book ready to pass into the professional hands of Ray Rhamey for interior design and e-book conversion. Thank you both, and thank you, Ray, for your critique and comments as well. As I said, it takes a village, and what a fine "village" I live in that has such people in it.

As a final note, I appreciate having found the book *DPs: Europe's Displaced Persons, 1945-1951* by Mark Hyman (1998), which provided statistical and factual information that fleshed out the backdrop of my story. It also verified tragic events that I only vaguely knew about at the time through eavesdropping on adult conversations, especially those involving suicide. I thank the author for devoting so much effort to weaving together with eloquence and compassion the complex strands of the DPs' harrowing passage through World War II and its aftermath.

About the Author

Hillevi Ruumet is a psychologist by training, a "psychonaut" by inclination. She has spent her adult life in the study and practice of Jungian psychology and dream analysis, cross-cultural spiritual traditions, and an integral approach to human development. The seeds of her career as psychologist, psychotherapist, professor of transpersonal psychology, workshop leader, and author were sown during her formative years as a child in the midst of World War II in Europe, evolving into a radical life transformation as an immigrant in New York City. *Under Fate's Wing* now tells this amazing story, which won the top writing prize in the memoir category at the 2014 San Francisco Writers' Conference.

Her education includes a B.A. from Mount Holyoke College, a Ph.D. in Clinical Psychology from Columbia University, as well as extended study and practice in Jungian and transpersonal psychology, Tibetan Buddhism, and mystical Christianity.

During the 1970s, she also became a pioneer in the then-emergent field of stress management and wellness. The varied strands of this journey evolved into the "map" of psycho-spiritual development she describes in her first book, *Pathways of the Soul* (2006).

She currently lives in Southern Oregon and, though retired from practicing psychotherapy, continues to explore and further the interdependent threads of spiritual and psychological development in herself and others. Her next writing project is still percolating.

Website: *hillevi-ruumet.com*
Blog: *blog.hillevi-ruumet.com*
Please visit.
You can also send e-mail to *hilleruu@gmail.com*

CPSIA information can be obtained at www.ICGtesting.com
Printed in the USA
BVOW02s1938170116

433249BV00007B/146/P